JOGGING ROUND MAJORCA

GORDON WEST was born in 1896. He studied at the London School of Economics and served in the Royal Navy in the First World War. After the war he began a career in journalism, at one time working as Editor of Publications for the Liberal party. He also toured the United States with two presidential candidates in 1928—Alfred E. Smith and Herbert Hoover—in order to study the progress of American elections for Lloyd George.

In the 1920s he was Foreign Correspondent for the *Westminster Gazette*, and during the years of the Second World War he was Foreign Editor of the *Daily Sketch*.

It was in the late 1920s that Gordon West and Mary, his wife, decided to explore the little-known island of Majorca, which was the inspiration for this book.

THE MERRY PEASANT

JOGGING ROUND MAJORCA

By

GORDON WEST

Illustrated By
WARWICK LENDON

Majorca is a golden island
Full of light and colour;
Land of dreams
A pearl enchanted,
Filled with splendour.

—*Hymn of Majorca.*

BLACK SWAN

JOGGING ROUND MAJORCA
A BLACK SWAN BOOK : 0 552 99601 7

Originally published in Great Britain by
Alston Rivers Ltd.

PRINTING HISTORY
Alston Rivers Ltd edition published 1929
Black Swan edition published 1994

This Black Swan printing
Copyright © Transworld Publishers Ltd., 1994

*We are delighted to be publishing our Black Swan
edition of this charming book and whilst every effort
has been made to discover the owner of the work
without success we would be pleased to hear from the
Author's estate.*

Black Swan Books are published by Transworld Publishers Ltd.,
61–63 Uxbridge Road, Ealing, London W5 5SA,
in Australia by Transworld Publishers (Australia) Pty Ltd.,
15–25 Helles Avenue, Moorebank, NSW 2170,
and in New Zealand by Transworld Publishers (NZ) Ltd.,
3 William Pickering Drive, Albany, Auckland.

Printed and bound in Great Britain by
Cox & Wyman Ltd., Reading, Berks.

TABLE OF CONTENTS

LIST OF ILLUSTRATIONS

FOREWORD

HAVING come late to Mallorca—these days the Mallorcans prefer the double L to the J—with one image in mind, I was totally unprepared for the variety of breathtaking scenery, the sea and the mountains, the secret and magical villages and towns in the interior, the hospitality and the Mallorquin cuisine ; they were all captivating, and made me anxious to read everything available about the island.

And in Blackwell's second-hand section on a wet Oxford Saturday I discovered this book, first printed in 1929 when jogging meant a leisurely progress rather than the determined physical effort of today. A quick flip through its pages told me that here was someone whose feelings about the island matched mine over sixty years later. Not a guide-book, but the account of an adventure, an escape from a rainy London to an island very few tourists had even heard of in those days, an island very largely much the same now as it was then when it comes to its natural beauty, its people and its places, its welcome and its charm.

Foreword

I read it from cover to cover in one sitting, so compelling and atmospheric was the narrative, so delightful and evocative the style, so vivid the reaction to the humour as well as the beauty, so real and appealing the characters portrayed; I knew at once that I wanted to share it with others by reading it on BBC Radio 4. Happily the Readings Editor and my Producer agreed. Now I'd had some pretty good reactions to programmes over the years, but nothing like the response this evoked. In fact second-hand bookshops throughout the country are probably still cursing me because of the number of enquiries they got from people who, having learned that the book was out of print, tried to locate a copy.

My resolve now was to get the book re-printed, so I was delighted when Black Swan agreed, as a result of which you are now able to read the full unabridged version of the book which captivated me and so many listeners—and those listeners have treats in store as they discover the wonderful chapters which I was obliged to leave out of the abridgement. I hope you will enjoy jogging round Mallorca as much as I did.

LEONARD PEARCEY

THE CALL OF THE SUN

CONSIDER for a moment the varying effects upon
the creatures of the earth, human and otherwise,
of the first ray of spring sunshine.

This particular ray was a very early ray. It was
born at a time when the trees of London were still in
mourning for the last year's descent of Persephone,
and not even the first pin-point of a green bud had
pierced through the blackness of the boldest and
most enterprising boughs.

It came through a window into a room in which
were five creatures : a man, a woman, a faithful retainer, a dog and a common house-fly in a state of coma.

The faithful retainer, who was the first to react
to the ray of sunshine, was engaged in those mysterious duties whereby faithful retainers invariably
contrive to make homes habitable for their mis-
tresses and intolerable for their masters. The
immediate effect of the ray upon her was to reveal
the partial omission of one of her sacred rites, concerning which the truly faithful retainer is always
punctilious. The omission may be expressed by her
own unsolicited confession that she had " scamped

her corners "; whereupon with considerable energy she proceeded to unscamp them, to the annoyance of the dog and the desperation of the man.

The dog, as an expression of his attitude towards the unscamping of corners, rose with weary resignation, stared about him hopelessly, and fastened his eyes for a while on the pool of sunshine. And suddenly he went to the open window, raised his head and sniffed vigorously; and having sniffed his fill he gave vent to his feelings, after the manner of dogs, by uttering the single and expressive word: *Wuff*. He then pattered to the door and begged before it in a manner calculated to touch the most unsympathetic heart; and upon its being opened he joyously fled forth and was lost, though his continued existence was presently made apparent by a clamorous disturbance inevitably associated with the canine pursuit of cats.

Whether it was the disturbance caused by the dog, or whether the vibration made by the unscamping of corners that roused the fly from its state of coma, cannot be recorded. Yet for some reason the fly did rouse himself, and crept weakly across a table into the pool of light created by the ray of sunshine, where he stopped awhile in profound meditation. And presently he began to show symptoms of sensuous pleasure, as flies will, by twisting and untwisting his fore-legs ; until suddenly he buzzed his irridescent wings and soared triumphantly ceilingwards, there to find Elysium in some warm corner, or to find a wife, or to find whatever joy flies do find in their own particular heaven.

We are left, then, with the man and the woman. They, too, went to the window and regarded the fuller sunlight outside, of which the ray was but a small part. And they betrayed signs of restlessness, even as the retainer and the dog and the fly. Then the man said to the woman :

" It's spring."

" Yes."

" Nuisance."

" Why ? "

" The old feeling ; the dog and the fly have it ; I have it too."

" I know. One wants to escape environment. One wants to find the sun, and adventures, and new faces, and new ideas, and new sights and sounds and smells, and new kinds of food to upset the system. Well ? . . . Lets ! "

" Now ? "

15

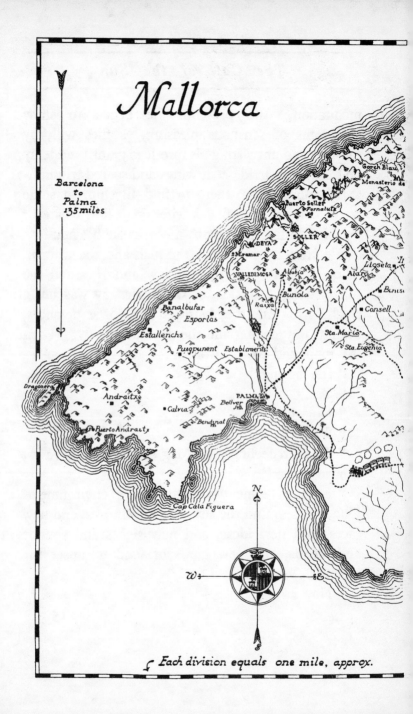

" Why not ? Next week."

" Where ? "

" Oh, somewhere "—dreamily said the woman, whom we will call the Spirit of Joy—" somewhere unspoiled, where people are still untouched by the influence of Freud and the devastating intellectuality of Hampstead, and where they haven't yet learned the connection between tweeds and tours. A place where smiles come from the heart and not from the pocket. A corner of Europe where people are so simple and unaffected that they will still kill you if they hate you and fall on your neck unrestrainedly if they love you."

" There has been no such corner in Europe," said the man, " since Mrs. Cook's small boy Thomas grew to maturity, married, and reared his family of adventurous sons."

" We will ask him," said the Spirit. So together they went and asked him—or maybe it was one of his sons—saying : " Tell us, if you please, of some places where you have no tours ; " and although he looked upon them as though he feared they might be insane, he after some difficulty discovered several such places, asking if these were enough and if that would be all to-day.

Now one of these places was Majorca, some say Mallorca, which is one of the Balearic islands in the Mediterranean Sea, called by the ancients Pityusae, or Islands of the Pines. It is inhabited by a hardy

race of peasants, the product of intermarriage between various types that include Carthaginian, Roman, Moorish, and Spanish ; it possesses a language of its own, Mallorquin, which has for its basis the old tongue of Catalonia ; it has a climate of the kind commonly called " ideal," which means that it is warm, sunny and dry if you go there during the warm, sunny and dry period of the year ; it has blue mountains, fertile valleys, orange and lemon

19

groves ; and its people retain · many of the ancient customs of their forefathers.

For this Elysian island, then, the man and the woman started, impelled, like the dog and the fly, by that first ray of sunshine.   And if, after you have explored the island with them, you do not find it to your liking, you must not blame them for wasting your time.

You must blame the ray of sunshine.

JOGGING ROUND
MAJORCA

I.—OUT OF PURGATORY

Now it is well known to all the world that the sunshine of northern Europe is a deceptive jade, that lures on the hopeful like a will-o'-the-wisp only to desert them when they are well and truly landed in some bog whence there is no escape. The mild sunshine that enticed away the man and the woman —whose identity will in future be disguised by the collective terms We and Us—most truly lived up to its character.

Came a morning when we were received into the echoing shelter of Victoria, a morning of leaden skies, hissing rain, and icy, boisterous wind, of shining wet mackintoshes, dripping umbrellas, grey faces, chilled and huddled bodies ; a morning when the windows of the train that bore us to the coast were blurred with rain, and the dreary sea, when we came in sight of it, was lashed to a savage whiteness by the tempest. Followed a voyage the agonies of which I forbear to describe, and an arrival that brought to three hundred tortured bodies a joy which even the lashing rain could not dispel.

" Of course," said the Spirit of Joy hopefully,

" it will have cleared up by the time we reach Paris.
It often does clear up before one reaches Paris. . . ."

But in Paris, where we made hurried journeys to
old haunts and old friends before we caught a night
train from the Quai d'Orsay, rain still swept the
streets, and the cold wind defied the thickest winter
overcoat.

" Undoubtedly," said the Spirit of Joy, still hopefully, " it will be fine when we get further south.
It always is finer when one gets further south. . . ."

Dawn, with the fair land of France still lashed by
the rain ; noon, with the city of Carcassonne in
flood ; two o'clock, and the Pyrenees are seen
mistily through the relentless torrent.

" Perhaps," began the Spirit, faintly, " it will——"

I stopped her firmly. " Let us have no more false
hopes. Let us anticipate at least a cyclone on the
other side. . . ."

Then among the Pyrenees and into the darkness
of the long tunnel by which we enter Spain. Desolate thoughts. Depressed spirits. We had come
too early. We had been lured away by the will-
o'-the-wisp into a South that was still in the grip of
winter. And even as despair began to descend upon
us the miracle happened. We emerged from the

tunnel into burning dazzling sunshine, into a land whose roads, covered with dust an inch in depth, had not known the touch of rain for a week. It was a startling transformation. On one side of the Pyrenees, Europe drenched with rain ; on the other, Europe warmed and dazzled by sunshine. The cloud of our depression lifted, and we faced the Spanish Customs with light hearts and open suit-cases.

The new Spain, the Spain of the Dictatorship, was forced to our attention even at the frontier station of Port Bou. Before the new régime, the traveller into Spain retained his passport ; now he must give it up entirely for half an hour while it is inspected, and then he must call for it, standing before an official who compares the photograph in the passport with the face of its claimant. And at the Customs inspection a new question is asked : " Have you any firearms ? "

The same atmosphere of suspicion we felt when we arrived at Barcelona, but then Barcelona has always been a restive, rebellious city, smouldering with sedition. The last time we were in Barcelona, soon after the end of the war, the rebellion-mongers were filling the streets with the fumes of their gas-bombs; and now, because they are held in check by a more competent Government, you can feel more strongly than ever the seething of their suppressed discontent.

When the train drew into the bare white station of Barcelona, we observed a large number of bright-uniformed men standing about in attitudes of splendid authority. They are not, as one might erroneously assume, the officials of the station, nor are they the civic powers assembled to greet you; they are policemen and Civil Guards. You have only to glance at a Spanish policeman to appreciate the need for the Civil Guards. The policeman is a slovenly fellow, in spite of his bright red and blue uniform; you may see him lounging against a wall, smoking a cigarette and chatting idly with a civilian crony. But the Civil Guardsman, in his blue-grey uniform and his shining, winged hat, with his rifle and revolver always ready for use, is a true symbol of power and efficiency. He radiates his consciousness of power; he is alert, masterful, aloof; never will you see him lounging or abating his incessant watchfulness by indulging in unnecessary conversation.

These men are awaiting our arrival. They inspect us, as they inspect everybody, with quick, searching

26

eyes. They inspect us so intently that they almost
succeed in convincing us that we have at least one
bomb concealed somewhere on our persons. We
wonder feverishly whether any of the literature
in our luggage could conceivably be regarded as
seditious literature. For the Civil Guards are ever
on the watch for Syndicalists, Bolsheviks, and
every kind of militant Socialist. I should not like
to predict what would happen to one who stood
before a Civil Guardsman and in a loud and triumphant voice cried " Karl Marx." The Guards have
not forgotten that a few years ago the Socialists were
tossing bombs about in the city almost as casually
as a visitor at a Zoo tosses buns to the bears. Conse-
quently the Guards are now inclined to be unreason-
able in matters of Socialism.

We safely passed their scrutiny, and in a few
minutes we were rattling over the stone-cobbled
streets of Barcelona in an hotel omnibus with
iron-shod wheels. Cobbles in contact with iron-
shod wheels do not make soothing music after a
journey of thirty-two hours, and when to the music
of cobbles in contact with iron you add the rattle
of glass windows loose in their frames, the last stage
of your journey becomes a torture.

27

It is an astonishing thing that every horse-drawn hotel omnibus in the world appears to have iron-shod wheels and windows that are loose in their frames. I mentioned this to the Spirit of Joy, and she, before sinking back into a plush corner—oh, the mockery of that plush!—with a finger in each ear, her teeth clenched, and her eyes closed, suggested that hotel omnibuses were made deliberately to produce this effect so that on arrival one would be too weary to observe the defects of the hotel.

The omnibus rattled on and on interminably over the stony streets, through streets shady with trees, and up the Rambla, that main street which is the pride of Barcelona. The Rambla is notable for the fact that it seems never to end. It goes on and on in a straight line, and even when it eventually ceases to be the Rambla and assumes an alias, it still goes on and on.

But what an example it is to the town-planners of the world! The usual order is reversed; the main part of the street, the centre, is paved, and edged with basket chairs, hundreds and thousands of them, stretching away and away through the city under the trees, where one may sit all day or sleep at night. On each side of this promenade, in a track scarcely

28

wider than a sidewalk, the one-way traffic passes, crowded, crushed, crawling along to its destination. Once a vehicle enters the up-stream it is trapped ; there is no turning back, although after the first half-mile a car may find an opening in the promenade where it is possible to cross into the downward stream.

This peculiarity proves especially useful to taxi-drivers when they are driving a stranger. You wish, perhaps, to go to the Hotel Splendiforous. Very well. The driver joins the upward stream and passes the first crossing place. A moment later you observe the Hotel Splendiforous on the other side of the street, served by the downward stream. But the taxi-driver would not hear of your getting out here—if you are a stranger ! He takes you on and on and on up the Rambla ; and then he enters the downward stream at the next crossing and takes you down and down the opposite side to your destination, which you passed ten minutes before. And then he expects gratitude to be expressed in your tip !

But if you are a pedestrian, you are a god. The whole street is made for you. The traffic on the sidewalks is a mere incident ; you feel towards the

29

traffic as a motorist, careering along an English road at forty miles an hour, feels towards the pedestrians who plod at the side in the swirl of the car's dust.

Our hotel proved to be on the Rambla, which is the site of most of the hotels in Barcelona. It has a lounge on the ground floor, looking on to the street, a café in front of the lounge, and a suave manager who appears to speak every language of Europe. He was so suave that he chilled our spirits when he greeted us in the vestibule. He has rooms—yes, he thought he could find room for us.

We are tired—he sees that. Not over the Rambla?—the noise? Ah, he is not sure, he cannot promise, but—he will try. He meditates a second.

Now it may have been nothing more than co-incidence, but while he meditated an hotel porter was quietly and unobtrusively smuggling our luggage upstairs. And a few minutes later the manager led us up to a room in which we found our luggage already deposited. It was a large, bare room divided into two parts by a wood and glass partition, thus having pretentions to a suite. The part in which were crowded the two beds, straw-stuffed and as hard as the Victorian horsehair sofa, was dark and chilly.

Was this all he had? Yes, quite all. And the price would be thirty pesetas a day, without meals—about a pound. We knew he was grossly over-charging; we knew that, having observed our weariness, he was taking advantage of it. But here was our luggage, full of the amenities of civilization. The thought of soap, the thought of water that was not full of coal, of pyjamas and clean clothes, was too much for us, and the cunning fellow knew it.

When Suavity had finished with us, Impudence took its toll of us. At the door next morning appeared the Catalonian boot-boy with my shoes. He pointed out that a lace was broken; could he replace it for the *señor*? Now, I had no recollection of having broken the lace in removing my shoes the previous night, but, assuming that in my eagerness to go to bed I might have snapped it—even though it was new a week before—I accepted his well-intentioned offer. The new lace cost one peseta fifty centimos, or about a shilling.

But when the boy appeared ten minutes later with the shoes of the *señroa* and pointed out that one of

the heels was hanging by its leather and would
surely cause the *señora* to break either her ankle or
her neck, or both, I felt justified in permitting the
small bud of suspicion to flower. I told him the
shoe had been brutally handled. He replied that
it would cost but six pesetas, and could be mended
in ten minutes if I would trust it to him. I said I
would never trust him again as long as he lived.
This, he intimated, would be a pity ; he would be
sorrowful for the rest of his days, but—in the
matter of that heel—

"What shall we do about it ? " I asked the
Spirit.

" Pull his ear," she suggested.

I pulled, and the owner of the ear departed,
loudly expressing his indignation at our ingratitude.

Outside the hotel, in the morning sun, we saw
through eyes strengthened by sleep that the Rambla
had several charms in spite of its noise. It has a
flower market in its centre, where women with their
ample proportions wrapped in shawls wade among
coloured seas of flowers on the pavement, and
endeavour to sell their blooms with a persistence
that is the special characteristic of flower-sellers
in every city in the world.

One reflects upon this, regretting, with a feeling of despair for humanity, that so much persistence should be required to sell beauty and fragrance, while no persistence at all is necessary to sell less beautiful things, such as plus-fours, whisky, tickets for sweepstakes or bad novels. It is difficult to imagine a vendor of whisky or Harris tweed following you out of the shop and up the street, pressing his wares against your cheek, holding them under your nose for you to smell, or to imagine yourself taking

33

pity on him, perhaps admiring his persistence, and saying, " Oh, very well, I'll have just *one*—a small one."

Next to the flower market is a bird market where hundreds of birds of every species and colour squawk, and twitter, and sing, and moult multicoloured feathers from innumerable cages. The bird-sellers have none of the persistence of the flower-sellers. They stand about negligently, without life or energy, and allow the birds to sell themselves ; a feat which the birds endeavour to accomplish by singing until their little throats attain bursting dimensions.

Up and down through this flower-and-bird market walk the men of Barcelona, furtive, sullen, suspiciously watchful and unshaven. Shaving appears to be a weekly event in Barcelona. Almost every man has a growth of several days on his face. There may be citizens who shave every day, though one presumes that they are so sensitive about their vice that they conceal it in the privacy of their homes. But the attention which the men of Barcelona fail to give to their faces is compensated by the care they lavish on the other end of themselves —their boots. Having your boots cleaned is one of the popular pastimes of Spain, but in Barcelona it is more than a pastime, it is a passion.

In the middle of the morning a business man, after an apéritif in his favourite café, goes into one of the many shops whose sole business is the cleaning of boots, sits in a red plush chair, lights a cigarette, opens his newspaper, and for five full minutes gives himself up to the exquisite enjoyment of having his footgear polished. After lunch he follows the same procedure; and in the evening, if he has strolled a few times up and down the Rambla, he has them cleaned again.

He sits in the plush chair, not with resignation, as one visiting a barber, but with conscious enjoyment; his face wears the expression of one who, having sipped the most perfect liqueur, is enjoying the knowledge that he still has three parts of the glassful to finish. Every street has its shoe-cleaning shop, and nowhere are you free from the youths who, carrying their cleaning paraphernalia and a foot-rest, inspect the minute particles of dust on your toe-caps, and accost you with the eternal cry " *Limpia botas, señor.*"

This passion for cleanliness of shoes is equalled by the passion for cleanliness of streets. Never a

35

swirl of dust comes spinning on the breeze to blind you and grit your teeth. No scraps of paper, torn newspapers or rubbish lie in the roadways. All day the barrels on wheels that are Spanish water-carts pass up and down refreshing the streets, and innumerable street cleaners in blue overalls, smoking their long cigars as they sweep, try to create a little dust for removal.

Barcelona possesses all the customary institutions needful to a self-respecting city. It has a cathedral, many churches, the cleverest pickpockets, several art galleries and museums, a bull-ring, and playing fields where youths perspire round a football under a July sun when the shade temperature is over 90 degrees. It has magnificent factories, a fine harbour, a battalion of cut-throats, and a splendid hospital ; a town mountain on whose heights you may pass the summer evenings, a casino where you may lose half your money to the tables and the other half to a pickpocket, and *cinemas de luxe* from whose screens the Gish sisters talk emotionally in subtitles of colloquial Spanish.

Yet, in spite of all these amenities of civilization, you cannot be happy in Barcelona. Even the English residents do not love Barcelona. It is an

36

unfriendly city, a place of commerce where the stranger is not wanted unless he has something to sell cheaply, or desires to buy. It is a restless, dissatisfied city, the Bad Boy of Spain. A city of furtive, mannerless men who eye your money-pocket or watch a woman's handbag like hungry animals. A city of slovenly, uncorseted, unbeautiful women whose eyes seldom smile, and in whose hearts there is no joy of life. Let us go on to Majorca.

But before we leave we must visit Tibidabo, the town mountain. Everybody who goes to Barcelona must visit the town mountain. It is a rite. We had a friend in Barcelona, and the first thing he said when we proposed to explore the city before leaving was : " Well, now, suppose you go up to Tibidabo." We asked an hotel guide what there was to see, and he replied : " Well, there is Tibidabo, *señor*— and the Cathedral." Appear with our shoes dusty and our faces moist with heat, and inevitably somebody will say, " Ah, you have been to Tibidabo ! " When a town mountain possesses so much importance, one cannot justify one's visit without making its acquaintance.

You reach Tibidabo by tram, barouche or taxi, and in so doing pass through the homes of the wealthy. Many of these pretentious palaces which line the long uphill route were built out of the riches gained in Spanish-American trade, and they express the mind of the Spanish *nouveau riche*. Each architect seems to have been in competition with a rival in his effort to produce a house of the highest rococo magnificence. Nowhere had we seen such a medley of strange structures in one road.

Here is one built to represent a house of rock as the architect imagines it would appear under the ocean. It is a large building with a façade of undulating, brownish imitation rock. The windows are partly covered from the top by slanting " eyelids " of the same tortured material, and give the house an air of being on the verge of dropping off to sleep. The whole surface of the house twists and writhes, as submerged objects twist and writhe in the eyes of a swimmer who gazes about him under water. One cannot but feel sympathy for the architect; to obtain his effects he must have spent many hours under water. But his eccentric creation is one of the prides of Barcelona; it has been enshrined on a postcard, like a musical comedy actress; and you find it undulating at you from every shilling packet of views.

Higher up the road to Tibidabo the architecture is even more mixed. Here is one house topped by two Mosque domes, façaded with Corinthian columns, and entered by a Bayswater portico! Here is another with ornate porphyry steps and purple sun shutters, its exterior walls decorated with dragon-like festoons of tiled flowers writhing roofwards. Here is a Moorish-looking structure guarded by ferocious blue china Oriental dogs. One marvels that these buildings should be found anywhere outside an Exhibition and Fun Fair. One almost expects a uniformed attendant to appear at a doorway with loud-voiced invitation to " come along, come along, see the lion-headed man and the fattest woman in the world."

Halfway up the slope of Tibidabo the tramway ends, and a funicular takes us the rest of the way. Although the journey occupies no more than ten minutes, the railway has first and second class coaches. The track is terrifyingly steep, and part of the way passes along the edge of a deep precipice.

A local gentleman of unusually swarthy aspect travelled up with us, looked at us, muttered to himself and immediately fell into a doze. When we reached the top of the mountain he awakened, alighted, sat on

a public seat, and fell into another doze. Later, when
we sat down at an ornate café of Oriental design, he
came across, sat at the table next to ours and dozed
again. When we returned to the funicular, he
travelled down in the same coach, and fell so fast
asleep during the ten minutes journey that he snored.

It was disconcerting to suspect that we had such
a soporific effect on him, but we consoled ourselves
with the thought that Tibidabo is intended above
all to be a place of rest and refuge from Barcelona.
It gives a magnificent view of the white city in the
plain beneath, surrounded by a ring of mountains
and faced by the shimmering, azure Mediterranean;
but when you have seen that, you have finished with
Tibidabo. And herein lies the reason for the
enthusiasm with which the citizens recommend
Tibidabo. There is nothing whatever to do there;
and the average Spaniard enjoys few things more
than having nothing whatever to do.

We went that afternoon to book two berths on
the boat for Palma. We had been told that it was
possible to obtain private second-class cabins for
two, but we had doubts about this, and our doubts
were now justified. There were, said the official—
a lean, dark-skinned fellow with a melancholy air—

only first-class private berths. He would advise us to travel first class. English *señors* and *señoras* always travelled first class, his manner informed us, and unless we travelled so, we could not be entitled to his respect. But at the risk of losing his respect we positively declined to travel first class.

He indicated that if we did not travel first class he could not promise that our lives would be safe while we slept; and when this failed he tried to sell us a guide-book, which seemed illogical since we were likely to die that night. Reluctantly at last he gave us the berths we required, though with mournful-eyed regret that we would not show ourselves to be truly high-bred by paying another hundred pesetas. . . .

And so to the boat—a toy steamer, snow-white and blue-funnelled, waiting at the quay-side in the dusk; fussing steamily as though eager to escape from Barcelona and find the Elysian islands. The Spirit stood on the quay amid the rabble of swarthy dock-rats, red-fezzed stokers, thieves, travellers, and loungers, policemen gorgeous in blue and red, Civil Guardsmen, hard-eyed and be-rifled, and she looked at the enthusiastic little craft almost with affection in her eyes, and she said:

41

" Why, the darling thing wants to go as much as we do ! "

She patted the tarry hull as though it were a dog, so that I half-expected the little boat to sit back on its rudder and bark ; and then, glancing at the palm of her hand, she asked me to lend her my handkerchief!

The darling thing, whose name was *Rey Jaime I* —glorious memory of that young giant of a king who wrested Majorca from the Moors—had for us a welcome which put Barcelona to shame.   The little man who stood at the end of the gangway could not be degraded with the name of steward ; rather was he a gentle-eyed, smiling elf of a host with a light of mischief behind his brown eyes and the manner of one who keeps open house.

" It's Lob—I'm sure it's Lob," said the Spirit.

He beamed at her and nodded vigorously, although he did not understand.   And indeed it might have been an incarnation of Barrie's queer little spirit, except that his legs were not spindly enough. There was the same air of mischievous secretiveness, as though he had queer and delicious things in store. You could imagine him slipping under the captain's bridge on hands and knees, weeping because he " needed to be loved " and there was nobody in

42

Barcelona capable of loving him. But the Spirit soon discovered that he had no reason to weep. Everybody on the little boat loved him at sight; and then there was the stewardess. Not quite the wife one would have chosen for him, the Spirit said; a little too buxom, a little puzzled always by his quaint fancies and his secret mischiefs; but still a loving and admiring wife even in her lack of understanding.

They led us below. And here—why did Lob hesitate, look at us with his head on one side, smile a little sadly, shake his head, and exchange a sympathetic glance with Mrs. Lob? Only because our ways parted, mine to the left, the Spirit's to the right! Eloquent, understanding Lob!

I had not been five minutes in the small white cabin with its four bunks, before there was a tap at the door and a small, excited face peered round.

" It *is* Lob," said the Spirit in a hushed voice. " He's sent me a flower by Mrs. Lob—look! . . ."

We sleep four in a cabin, women on one side of the ship, men on the other. The cabins are white and clean as the rest of the boat, with embroidered counterpanes and curtains of golden-brown. Already one of the lower bunks was occupied by a fat Catalonian merchant who, despite the lowness of

43

his bed, climbed into it with many grunts and at
once fell into a state of oblivion which was signified
by the gentle whistle of his snore.

The occupant of the bunk above him was a little
Majorcan who had the greatest difficulty in attaining
his couch. First he tried to mount from the small
movable stand provided for the purpose, but this
was not high enough. Then he tried to pull
himself up by his arms, but these were not strong
enough. At last, by a series of jumps, he succeeded
in throwing his body face down across the bunk ;
but then his legs became unmanageable. They
dangled down and waved pathetically around the
cabin, like the antennæ of some insect emerging
from its hiding-place. Desperate attempts he made to
pull them in, first drawing up one and then the other
in an effort to grip the side of his bunk with his knees.

His breathing became feverish. Suddenly the
mattress began to slide out ; he uttered a strangled
cry of despair, clutched frantically but futilely at
the air, and fell with a crash to the cabin floor,
mattress and sheets atop of him. The fat Catalan
awoke with a yell, muttered ill-temperedly, turned
over, and resumed his whistling. The head of the
little Majorcan emerged from the tangle of bed-

clothes, and he laughed. Merry soul! I helped him up when he had rearranged the bed, and then I went on deck to find the Spirit.

The lights of Barcelona were no longer visible. Three young priests, thin, ardent ascetics, stood silently gazing with luminous eyes and parted lips at the dark horizon behind us where Spain lay. A full moon in the south, pointing a pathway of shimmering silver across the Mediterranean to the other horizon where hide the Elysian islands. A white fairy boat, surging along that silver pathway, breaking it, and scattering the remnants behind in a million dancing jewels. A great hush of silence. . . .

45

II.—INTO PALMA

THE nasal instrumentalism of the fat Catalan, which had begun in excellent imitation of a tin whistle, developed during the night into the lower note of a piccolo ; and at dawn, after having attained a saxophonic crescendo, it terminated in an explosive outburst that awakened me for the fourth time. Followed the crackling of thick dry lips being moistened with a tongue ; the questioning mutter as heavy eyes opened on uncomprehended surroundings ; the grunt of disgust as a dissatisfied mind merged into full consciousness ; the sound of swirling bedclothes ; then silence, and once again that faint, thin whistle of a Catalonian soul at peace.

But the musician earned my gratitude by awakening me, for the porthole framed a deep black outline of the hilly coast of Majorca merging from a sheet of ruffled silver, and I went on deck. On the way, in the bare saloon, I met Lob, making pleasant music with cups, and from a dwarfed doorway that could have been built for nobody but Lob came the rejuvenating odour of strong coffee. A few deck passengers still lay sleeping on their hard couches ;

47

here a Spanish trooper with his head pillowed on
a coil of rope, over which his open mouth sent a
dribble of saliva; there a young peasant farmer
half-hidden under the ship's donkey engine. The
three ardent-eyed priests were there, silent and
motionless, gazing astern as though they had never
changed their position since the previous night.
Up in the bows of the ship a dark-hued peasant girl
watched with glowing eyes the dark coast-line,
crooning to herself a soft melody which we afterwards found to be one of the folk songs of Majorca.
One glance I had of the dark mountain rising out
of the sea, silhouetted by the first promise of the
sunrise; then I went back to rouse the Spirit.

The Majorcans will tell you that there is no dawn
so beautiful as that which awakens Majorca from
her ocean slumber. Half the passengers in the ship
gather to watch the sun come up out of the sea at
the end of those shadow-blackened hills. As the
pale yellow flush merges into gold their chatter dies
away, and the glow of the dawn reflects in the wide
watching eyes. Many times they have seen the
dawn creep from the sea, yet each time it is a new
wonder to them. They are hushed to breathless-
ness as the gold is suffused with rose, and an edge

THE PATH TO THE MOUNTAINS

Facing page 48

of fire creeps along the tops of the mountains. And then, when the first crimson fragment of the sun rises out of the water, they exhale their breaths with faint exclamations of satisfaction, ecstasy, even relief; as though they might have feared that for once the sun would forget Majorca.

An hour later we entered the Bay of Palma. To the incoming traveller the very shape of the city constitutes a welcome. It is built low on the plains round the bay, shielded at the back by a ring of mountains; and the circling arms of its crescent extend to receive you, and finally they embrace you and take you to the heart of Palma.

Then the behaviour of the little boat *Rey Jaime* impresses you. She steams herself into a flurry, turns her nose in the direction of Palma's greatest treasure—the Cathedral by the Sea—and hurries towards it. She seems to be joined in a pleasant conspiracy with the city of Palma, for while the circling arms embrace us, the *Rey Jaime*, after giving three loud shrieks of triumph, takes us straight to the great cathedral and drops us almost at its door; as though, having captured us, she is eager to give us the finest of first impressions by landing us at the feet of her greatest treasure.

51

Surely the Cathedral of Palma has one of the finest situations of any cathedral in the world. Its foundations are almost washed by the waves, and it is separated from the ocean only by the ancient wall of the city and a narrow coast road. It draws the eye as soon as the boat rounds the hills and gives the first sight of Palma; it holds the eye as the boat approaches; the city around and behind it becomes nebulous, a thing of insignificance, a splash of white out of which towers this vast rose-tinted creation of Gothic grace and beauty. Like a mother she stands there by the ocean's edge, and like children the buildings of the city gather behind and at her sides: a perfect symbol of the Church she represents.

The *Rey Jaime*, having brought us to her Cathedral, uttered another triumphant shriek that echoed and reverberated among the mountains, and in her exuberance bumped violently into the quay, so that many passengers unexpectedly assumed sitting positions on the decks. No harm done, but rather good, for the laugh that rose from the shore joined with the laugh that went up from the boat; and the day that begins with a laugh at 6 a.m. holds infinite promise. A little group of islanders stood on the

quay, most of them women who had come down to
greet their men returning from trading expeditions
in Barcelona. They were shawled and hatless,
with faces full of contentment and breaking into
smiles ; at once you can see from their expressions
that this is an island of peace and goodwill.

And then we noticed the remarkable absence of
policemen in red and blue and of Civil Guardsmen
with rifles and revolvers. Nowhere could we see
anybody dressed in the garments of official importance ; not even a Customs official paraded his
uniformed glory. But as soon as the gangways
established connection with the boat we found that
there was at least one official presence. He was a
mild, smiling, and extremely apologetic little man
wearing a cap, and he stood at the end of the gangway
to inspect passports.

" How he hates doing it," the Spirit said.

And so it seemed. Every gesture told us that he
would refrain from this absurd interference with our
liberty if he could ; since he could not, would we
bear with him just for a moment while he wrote
down in his little notebook the name of the country
to which we belonged ?

He was puzzled by my passport. He did not

know such a country, he said. He was sorry, he was apologetic, but—where *was* this country? If I would inform him, so that he could write it down in his notebook. He had his finger on an inscription, and I saw that he was pointing to "Birthplace : Guildford, Surrey."

I explained that Guildford, Surrey, was not a country, but a small town in a country called Inglaterra. Ah, he knew Inglaterra! He wrote the name in his little notebook, and then, when the Spirit offered him her own special passport—for she is an independent Spirit and has one of her own —he raised his cap and declined to bother her, so long as she would assure him that she also came from the same country.

We had already chosen one of several hotels on the strength of its boast of "running water in every room." To this hotel we proceeded without delay in a Majorcan hackney carriage. Now the Majorcans are individualists, and this carriage was the first expression we had of their individualism. It resembled more than anything else a country baker's cart. It had two tall wheels, a yellowish hood supported by an arched frame, a small window at each side of the hood, and was drawn by two horses

54

side by side. It was a light cart and did not need
two horses, but the Majorcan hackney driver likes
to make a show of his equine possessions. He sat
on the front of the cart while we established ourselves under the hood, feeling like a pair of loaves
about to be delivered. We saw many of these
hooded carts standing in ranks, each with its two
horses, plying for hire. If a driver, thinking you a
likely fare, wishes to attract your attention, he
cracks his whip at you ; and if he fails to win you,
he smiles and rolls himself another cigarette.

Our two horses rattled through the awakening
streets of Palma at a good speed ; up the wide
avenue beside the Cathedral and the Lonja and the
Almudiana palace of the Moors ; along the wider
streets to the narrow ways in the centre of the town.
It stopped at a wide archway, which was the front
door of our hotel, in a street so narrow that it might
have been a long corridor whose roof had been
removed.

Beyond the archway was a dim tiled hall, chilly
as a tomb, containing a few chairs and a locked piano
covered with a white embroidered muslin coat.
Above the piano hung the life-size photograph of
an excessively fat and smiling young girl. Of whom

55

more later; for her death, three months before, engendered one of the most scandalous subterfuges ever practiced by the Spirit on a disagreeable human being.

A lean, melancholy young man in a white coat leads us up a wide, winding stone staircase to the top of the house. One room that he shows us we reject because it is filled with the rumble of carts from the stony street below. Another we take. With food it will cost but eight pesetas a day each, or about five shillings.

It has two small white iron bedsteads, counterpaned with pale yellow; it has bare white-washed walls and a black-and-white tiled floor; two chairs, no cupboards, a window three feet by two, tucked away in a corner as by an afterthought, and a fixed washbasin with running water.

There is trickery in this running water. True, it runs in, but after it has been used refuses to run out. We pointed this out to the lithe gypsy of a young woman who presently brought us coffee, and she deplored it. She took a hairpin from her head and ineffectually poked it down the pipe.

This modern nonsense, it was always bringing trouble, she said. How much easier, how much more sensible, how much less trouble to have a bowl that you could empty into a pail and carry downstairs. She probed and swirled and clicked with the hair pin, but hopelessly; it was a futile fight against modernism, which finally conquered her. . . .

Refreshed after the coffee, we went out into the street where the carts were rumbling. They were country carts returning empty, and we argued that if we walked in the direction whence they came we should find the market.

It proved to be at the end of the narrow street, which is one of the main thoroughfares of the town. As we approached, a sound that had been a distant murmur grew into a hoarse roar, and soon we could distinguish it as the sound of many voices. Two thousand Majorcans were talking in the market-place as only Majorcans can talk : loud, animated, full-throated talk, without reserve and with a hundred gestures to aid its flow! Talk about everything and nothing, a cataract of talk that bewilders like the roar of a great waterfall ! Talk in two languages, Spanish and Majorcan, unceasing from dawn to sunset. Talk that obliterates the rumble of carts and drowns our voices when we shout into each other's ears.

We stand bewildered by the noise, dazzled by the blinding, relentless sun in the big white square. Here are rows and rows of stalls, covered by awnings and shaded at the sides by hanging white cloths to hold off the sun. Stalls dangling with crimson ropes of dwarf tomatoes, like necklaces for giants' wives; piled with mountains of green peas, with yellow sierras of oranges and lemons and nespolis, with socks and tapes, with coloured handkerchiefs, shawls and string-soled shoes, with meat and fish— such fish as you find guarded and prized in aquariums, here displayed for sale to be slapped into a rush bag and cooked for the evening meal.

There are fish beautiful and ugly ; little red fish with yellow eyes ; ink-fish, squid-like creatures the colour of a bruise, with dying tentacles that cling and suck at the stone slabs on which they lie ; silvery minute fish, like sticklebacks, in tumbled heaps, some still gasping for breath and feebly curling a tiny tail ; more fish, with snarling, sharkish mouths and with mouths round and mournful.

There is fascination in a Mediterranean fish market ; it has so infinite a variety of sea creatures that we can never gaze upon them without feeling that we are in an aquarium. Here you will find none of the fish that you are accustomed to see on the marble slabs of the English fishmonger : there are no doleful cod, no dried, headless haddock, none of the characterless creatures of the northern seas.

Here the fish have two distinct characteristics : they are sinister, or they are beautiful. The big lobsters, the red mullet, the silvery midget fish— these give colour to the market ; the ink-fish and a species of miniature shark supply the sinister note. Many of them are still alive, for they have just been brought up from the fishing boats. The dying tentacles of a bluish squid slither feebly over the stone slab, and presently one of the chattering fishwives, for our delectation, gives the creature a resounding slap on its body. Its colour turns from bruise-blue to purple, its eyes stare at us accusingly with helpless indignation, and its tentacles tremble in futile menace !

Then comes he of the melancholy eyes who had received us at the hotel ; he is buying fish, ink-fish. The fishwife discerns that we are to be the guests of his house, and with a quick smile at us she gives him the fish she has slapped, so that we shall feel a greater intimacy with our food !

We pass on and meet the garlic vendor, who

59

would have us buy.   She is aged, fat, bronzed by the
sun, and wears the voluminous black skirt and the
shawl that form the national costume of Majorca.
The white, evil-smelling bulbs hang in strings round
her neck and across her shoulders, like knotted
Medusan tresses.   Her body smells of garlic, her
breath smells of garlic, she is garlic outside and in,
and likely enough her home is festooned with garlic
hanging to dry.

Groups of bare-headed peasant women in their
black shawls, the younger ones with two pigtails of
hair down their broad backs, go their daily round of
inspection.   Some of them wear little white net
coifs at the back of their heads ; others, town-bred
and more sophisticated, throw over their heads
small black veils that are like timid imitations of the
mantilla.   The white coif is the distinguishing mark
of the peasant women, but the black head-veil
signifies a higher status of island society.

Lean yellowish hounds, whose ancestors hunted
for the ancient Egyptians and came to Majorca with
the Phœnicians, slink with lithe, unhurrying pace
among the stalls, seeking what they may devour.
Like pale ghosts of dogs they are, whom no amount
of food will fatten ; melancholy, sensitive ghosts

that shrink from us and will not tolerate a caress. Mules stand impassive, waiting for their panniers to be filled, sometimes lowering their heads to sniff at the questing hounds.

The human vitality of this market weakens us. We feel feebly ineffectual, midgets swept up into a great vortex of sound and energy and unceasing activity. It is the vitality not only of a Latin people, but of a vigorous island people, bred of the soil and the sea, untouched by the civilization of cities.

We passed out at the far side of the Plaza Mayor, and began a little to recover our strength. Here, at one side of the market, are the pottery sellers, and at sight of them the Spirit's eyes brighten and she darts forward like an eager bird that has seen a pile of crumbs.

" Peasant pottery. Oh, we must have some ! Look—this glorious primitive plate."

She produced it from a pile, a large rough-shaped piece with the unevenness that shows the hand of the primitive potter ; a lemon-coloured plate with rough splashes of jade. Another she finds of a rich brown with yellow markings like Arabic symbols. She goes through the pile of plates like a card-shuffler, and the pottery vendor becomes

61

interested, then catches a little of the enthusiasm and herself begins to shuffle pottery, displaying other pieces which she thinks might attract the Spirit. A little crowd of curious people begins to gather behind us, puzzled that we should excite ourselves over the cheap rough ware that is in common use in the Majorcan kitchens, and unable to see the beauty of its primitive crudity and its simple decorative effects.

It has the charm of all peasant pottery; it is so obviously made for utility, yet even so the creator must needs give each piece its rough dash of colour. The favourite colours are lemon and deep red-brown, and the decorations are splashed on with a careless brush. The larger utensils of the kitchen are of red, unglazed pottery, and their shape and design are the same that you will find in the museum of Pompeii, or in the household of the Sicilian.

I have to warn the Spirit that we have other days for shopping, and promise her a real pottery hunt later.

" But I must have just *one* to-day," she says, " so that I can feel I've really got one."

Lemon and jade is cheap at thirty centimes, so we buy it, just for the joy of possession, and wander

on. We have not gone far before a policeman in
a cambridge-blue uniform, smoking a cigarette,
stops me with semi-serious reproof, and we discover that we have broken the town's rule of one-way
pedestrianism ! *Down* one side of the street, *up*
the other—that is the law. But, we ask, if we are
on the down side and wish to visit a shop on the up
side—what then ? Ah, then one crosses, but after
one's business is finished one goes over to the other
side again ! There is never any congestion in these
streets, and at no time is there much traffic ; still,
you must keep to your side, even if you are the only
human creature in the street !

They have some good small shops in Palma,
several of them of an elegance worthy of Paris or
London. But the women's shops—the milliners
and the gown establishments—are devoid of style ;
they have no *chic ;* they are the kind of shop you
find in the small country towns in England. For
there are so few women in Majorca, even in the
capital, who wear anything but the national shawl,
that there is little demand for hats and gowns. Here
is a hat shop which the Spirit has found. She found
it because there was a crowd of hatless women round
its window. Whenever we see women grouped

63

round a Palma shop window, we know now that it must be a hat shop. These hatless women cannot resist hats, although they can never wear them.

This window displays a dozen hats, simple, unpretentious objects without character or originality. The unhatted women stand and gaze at each creation—they are interested with an unquenchable feminine interest; yet they will die without ever feeling that exquisite consciousness of being perfectly hatted.

We pass a tobacco booth situated close to the office of the state lottery; and I am reminded of my need for cigarettes. The Majorcans stock all the pungent brands of Spanish cigarettes, but they have also a kind peculiar to Majorca, which are smoked mainly by the peasants. The Spirit soon found a name for them: she calls them " The Outfitter's Friend " because of the damage they do to my clothes. If you value your garments, then avoid the Majorcan cigarette. Its covering is a heavy white paper, thick as notepaper; it is rolled but not stuck down at the edge; and the coarse paper is tucked in at each end to hold in the black crumby tobacco: like a herb cigarette for the asthmatical.

They require a good deal of manipulative practice before you can smoke them in safety. When you apply a match the bunched paper tucked in at the end is liable to flare up like dry grass, to the detriment of your eyebrows ; and even if you should avoid this peril, you must always be on the alert for fear you lose your tobacco, which may shoot out in a black Niagara over your clothes, leaving you a hollow tube of paper between your lips. Sometimes the tobacco chooses to travel in the opposite direction : you indulge in a self-satisfying inhalation and the crumby, bitter interior of the cigarette shoots into the back of your throat ! With patience you will in time master these cigarettes ; but you will never grow to like them. Their flavour is a mixture of burning paper and smouldering leaves, and they require relighting with a frequency that plays havoc with your stock of matches.

By this time we had reached the Casa Consistorial —the City Hall of Palma—in an open space that is the meeting place of three of the principal streets of the city. It is also the meeting place of the old men of Palma. All round the front of it they sit, on a long stone ledge in the sun. They are bright-eyed old men in whose faces lies the great peace that we see and feel everywhere among the Majorcans. Their countenances are beautiful with peace. These are the faces of men who have the consciousness of peace well merited after centuries of battling for the freedom of their island.

Consider their troubled history. First came Mago, brother of Hannibal, slaying and destroying; then the legions of Rome, conquering, rebuilding and strengthening; followed the Vandals, burning and ravishing, and the Moors, who sacked the city and carried off the most beautiful of her women, afterwards making Palma one of the seats of their Mediterranean power.

Again the voice of battle along the circling bay, when Rey Jaime Conquistador, that giant of a boy, won back the island and so became the hero of Majorcan history. Wars and more wars, even in the last century, when the Majorcans suffered so severely in the Cuban war that as a reward for their age-long heroism they were exempt from all further service in the conflicts of Spain. That reward has been taken from them now, but to the aged men Majorca is still an island that has won her peace in the world.

Watch them here, with the chill blood of their old age warmed by the sun, in this street that has been stained crimson with the blood of their ancestors ; a medley of races whose types are so clearly defined that we can say : Here is a Roman, there a Mauretanian, and here a pure-blooded Castilian from Spain. Their bright youth-flashing eyes reflect our curiosity, and as we pass old head leans towards old head while we in our turn are discussed.

One of them, an old, lean man with clean complexion the colour of sandstone and a fine aquiline nose, wears the national costume of the men of Majorca. He has a broad-brimmed, black Spanish hat set straight upon his head, such a hat as poster artists delight to give us on our hoardings in England. Over his shoulders hangs a voluminous black cloak reaching almost to his ankles, and beneath this we glimpse a short, close-fitting embroidered vest. But the trousers are his chief pride. They are full and baggy, like the trousers of a Turkish woman, and they reach to his calves, where they are fastened round his black stockings. Yards of material have gone to their making. When he walks they surge around his legs like a pair of pleated skirts.

These trousers, which are relics of the Moorish occupation, are seldom seen in the island now. The men have taken to the less picturesque coat and trousers of the civilized European ; the broad hat and Eastern trousers are preserved for ceremonial occasions, for festas and national celebrations.

The old man is conscious of his costume ; he walks away slowly, with a serene dignity, giving to an acquaintance whom he passes a salute worthy of some benevolent aristocrat.

We turn our attention again to the row of old men, for we have a special interest in them. Whenever we enter a new country we first make a study of the old people and the young women, because we find that they give us the truest indication of the conditions of their country. Where we see young wives listless or sullen or uninterested, and old men weary and dull-minded under the burden of their years, we know that we may expect discomfort in our lodgings, dirtiness, poor food, and often discourtesy. But here we expect none of these things ; the old men are still vigorous and keen, and their eyes have a kind of bird-like brightness that indicates the liveness of their faculties, while the women everywhere are smiling, busy, and interested in their busy-ness.

This is one of the secrets of their contentment, the vivid interest and the pride they have in their own busy-ness. Theirs is not a listless, grudging toil, undertaken only because it is compulsory; it is a toil that has in it something of the spirit of the artist, who finds a joy in his labours. Seldom will you see here a sullen worker, though you will find many who sing while they toil.

We came at last back to the cold cavernous entrance to our hotel and went in search of food. We were hungry, for we had been wandering the narrow maze of Palma's streets since eight o'clock that morning. Normally, after a journey extending over nights and days, you are not inclined for immediate explorations, but the voyage from Barcelona to Palma is so restful—provided you have a calm sea—that you may begin explorations without delay.

At the hotel, he of the melancholy eyes greeted us sadly and led us to a table in the dining-room. It was separated from the cold cavern by a wood and glass partition, and opened on to a small patio or courtyard. The walls were coloured a bright yellow up to within two feet of the ceiling, then came a fantastic frieze of dark green hills and valleys full of cypress trees.

The menu showed a curious mixture of French,

Spanish, and Majorcan. It began with *entremesses variados,* the equivalent of hors d'œuvres, consisting of anchovies, radishes and potatoes speckled with chopped onion. Then followed *arroz paella*—a strange-looking dish. The Spirit examined it with a frown of perplexity; then she drew back, startled, and looked at me.

"I can't eat it," she said. "I can't possibly eat it. It's the inkfish that was slapped!"

I should hardly have recognized it except for the pathetic tentacles, now lying in the stillness of a stewed death and masquerading under another name. It was companioned by sea crustaceans, by mussels pink and black, lying exposed in their shells. The tentacles twined in and out amid boiled rice saturated with brown gravy; here and there flared the red of tomato.

I urged the Spirit to try the mixture, but she was immovable. The ink-fish was too much for her. To eat a creature that had been slapped in its death agony for her amusement; to bite into tentacles that had trembled with impotent menace and been powerless to retaliate; to swallow a body that had turned purple with indignation at the unprovoked assault; to nourish herself with eyes—yes, perhaps

70

eyes, she said—that had stared at her with dying accusation—it was too much for the Spirit! But I, brute that I may be, forgot the accusing eyes, the flushing body, the impotent threat of the tentacles. I ate, and I enjoyed.

The ink-fish was a novelty to my taste: it had a soft insidiousness that at first I could not define. It had little resemblance to fish, but tasted more like—let me, out of consideration for the very genteel, say it in a whisper: it tasted rather like that much despised, that terribly plebeian offal, tripe.

Followed *fidcot à la Parisien*, a mixture of macaroni, onion, and scattered scraps of breast of mutton. Then *medlan merlan*—a red fish with tartar sauce; *ragoût de ternera*, a stewed nondescript meat with fried potatoes and peas sprinkled with chopped green herbs. The next item, *alcachofas catalane*, proved to be artichokes stewed with onions. Finally came a *dulce*—caramel custard; a basket piled high with the fruit of the island—oranges, cherries, nespolis, and bananas from the Canaries, and wine, unlimited wine of the country, thrown in with the meal; one bottle, two bottles if we wish. This common wine of Majorca is of two kinds: one rich, heady and fruity, the other highly flavoured with water and having a slightly acid bite. And everywhere it is given free and unlimited ; in the smallest country *fonda* we found later that no sooner had we finished a bottle between us than another appeared on the table.

The abundance of food in a Majorcan meal is overpowering. It is impossible to eat even a half of all that is set before us.. Even in the country places, as we discovered later, the meals are enormous ; but they are simpler, and unspoiled by the liquid sewage that for some reason infects the hotel cuisines in the capital.

In the country *fondas*, lamb cutlets form the staple dish ; they gave us lamb cutlets with nearly every meal ; for one of the industries of the island is the rearing of sheep, and great numbers of the lambs are killed off in their early youth. Fish, too, was plentiful everywhere ; beautiful red mullet, tunny fish, whiting, even lobster we had in some of the inns after we left Palma. The simple food of the country people delighted the Spirit, who cannot tolerate the high-flavoured disguises in which good food is masqueraded for the delectation of the foreigner.

Sometimes they give you with the fruit a selection

of Majorcan pastries. They have a genius for pastries. The crust is finer and richer than the finest shortbread, but sometimes the concealed contents of the tarts and puffs are disconcerting. One may contain jam : that is good. Another may be stuffed with green herbs : to appreciate this a specially educated palate is necessary. Your *dulce* may sometimes consist of a quarter of a pound of damson cheese, which is made in large quantities and is on sale in many of the shops. . . .

*   *   *   *   *

The other occupants of the dining-room where we had our first meal were not particularly interesting ; most of them were visiting Spaniards, men of business, who ate with nonchalant speed and left as soon as they had finished their meal.

The hotel proprietor came up to our table to make our acquaintance. He is a little, lithe Majorcan, black-clothed, with black hair and watchful dark eyes. Are we well nourished ? Yes, exceedingly. Shall we be staying long ? We are not certain, perhaps a week before we go into the interior ; afterwards no doubt we shall return here. He will be pleased to give us any information we may require. He bows and glides himself away black-cattishly.

We decided that afternoon to look down upon the
city of Palma from the slopes of El Terreno, the
residential district on the hills around the western
shores of the bay.   To reach El Terreno we passed
through the fisherman's quarter of the city.   Our
path twisted through a maze of alleys enclosed by
dwarf houses that dazzle the eyes with their whiteness in the sunshine, and here we had our first
glimpse of Majorcan hospitality.

We were displaying an architectural interest in a
small house that had a fine Moorish doorway and
brilliant green sun-shutters over its windows, when
a little girl who was sitting on the doorstep rose and
came shyly towards us.   She was eating a slice of
something that looked like bread and honey, from
which she had already taken several large bites;
her mouth was sticky with the honey.   She stopped
within a yard of us, smiled, and offered her slice to us.

Now it is the custom for Majorcans to offer to
the stranger a share of their food.   Many times
during our later explorations of the island we were
offered this hospitality, but we never accepted it,
because we learned our lesson from the little girl
who extended to us her bread and honey.

In all innocence, because we wished to show our

friendliness and to avoid hurting her feelings, we
thanked her, took the slice and had each a small
nibble.

The girl watched us, and when the second nibble
had been taken a most disconcerting change came

over her face. Her brown eyes opened wide and
her mouth drooped at the corners; then her lips
quivered and suddenly she burst into tears.

75

Clearly we had blundered. Her offer had been a mere gesture of welcome; she had not intended that we should accept it. She was merely conforming to the custom of her people. We hurredly returned her slice, whereupon the tears ceased and she smiled again. We left her happily consuming the rest of the slice.

Once out of the fishermen's quarter the character of Palma changes. The hillside over the blue bay is built upon with formal white villas, many of them having beautiful terraces, gardens full of red geraniums, and purple bourgainvillea climbing the walls. Here you will see the influence of the English colony—in the houses, in the few shops, and in the Hotel Mediterraneo that hangs on a ledge of rock in the cliffs.

High above, the old thirteenth-century castle of Bellver rises out of the pine-woods that cover the mountains. We climbed the rocky path through these woods, crossed the deep dry moat of the castle, and ascended one of the towers by the winding stone stairs.

From the weather-worn battlements we watched the sun set on Palma. The mountains behind the city darken, turn black; wispy clouds tinted with rose rest in the air above; the blue of the bay merges into a deep purple, and between the purple of the sea and the blackness of the mountains Palma lies, a city of silver-white jewelled with lights. . . .

And now we are tired. We want to sleep. The air is so soft up here that we could sleep soundly on the rocks at our feet. Let us go down through the dim pine-woods and along the white road, back to the yellow counterpanes that cover that blessed paradise, bed!

*　　*　　*　　*　　*

Because this volume is the personal record of a journey, I do not propose to inflict a detailed account of all the works of art, all the church architecture, all the historic palaces that we explored in Palma. Rather do I wish to convey an impression of the soul of the island, the character of its people, their habits and their customs; and to this end I shall tell chiefly of our adventures and of the personalities that we encountered in Majorca.

Yet I cannot pass to personalities without brief attention to the old palaces of the dead and dying Majorcan families. Many of them are reminiscent of the old palaces of Florence: buildings with

77

massive iron-studded doors shutting off the *patio* from the street, relics of the days when the steely hiss of sword against sword sounded in the streets and blood was cheap as wine.

Refuges from all the terrors of the streets were these old palaces, where a man could find safety almost in the face of a battering ram. But now the doors are thrown wide, and you may pass into the *patio* and linger at the fine wells that raise their carved stone sides and wrought metal-work from the paved floors. You may walk up the slanting staircase of carved stone along the side of the *patio* to the main door, and, if you are courteous, may be graciously shown through the high rooms.

You may see walls hung with some of the finest work of Murillo and Rubens and Velazquez. You may see rooms rich with damasks and tapestries and the exquisite blue and white Majorcan linen which has been made for centuries by singing, contented peasants. Sometimes you will find in a garden the relics of past conquerors, as the Arab baths : crumbling, silent ruins of ineffable beauty.

Here is the house of a famous Majorcan count, who only a few years ago died in poverty after he had ruined himself by backing the bills of his

78

dearest friends. Here is a church where, more than four hundred years ago, the local Montagus and Capulets met in pious devotion, quarrelled in the middle of the service, drew swords, called for partisans, and left the church—a few of them—only when its aisles were piled high with three hundred dead and dying. In every street, almost in every house in Palma, there is romance, gay and tragic, for those who seek it.

But in time even the romance of an historic city exhausts itself. We drift for a while into dreams of the past, bright-coloured dreams wherein the ghosts of kings and knights, troubadours and beautiful women pass before our eyes, walk with us in the streets and surround us when we enter their homes. Then comes the inevitable reaction when, surfeited, we awaken to a craving for actuality, for human and more vital contact.

Ghosts are truly charming creatures, and so very tractable and accommodating; they come when we beckon and depart when we will them to depart; and perhaps for this reason they tire us. They deny us the condiment of conflict which gives so much flavour to life. Let us leave them, then, and search instead for flesh and blood, creatures living and human.

79

Come with us first down to the old sea wall and see the Human Spider at his work. It is a magic day for wandering.

A sky cloudless and blue ; a sea of slow-ruffling azure ; a soft breeze stirring the palm trees by the old Alcazar of the Moors ; circling mountains misted in a smoke-blue haze of heat. We sing as we wander, for we are beginning to feel now the exquisite peace of Majorca, that divine content which fills the heart with music.

Here on the sea-road, in the shadow of the cathedral, the Human Spider—for so we christen him—spins from palm fibre the string which is so necessary to the daily life of the Majorcans. They make their shoe-soles with string, closely wound and compressed in two or three layers, and the seats of their chairs, and often the curtain coverings for their open doorways.

The Human Spider works in a stretch of land about a hundred yards long. We call him the Spider because he spins as he walks, leaving behind him a line of perfect thread. He is so dexterous that he spins a yard of thread every second, so that in a minute and a half he has left behind him more than a hundred yards of thread. At his waist, swathed round and round his body until he looks like a walking cocoon, he carries a bundle of grassy fibre, like coarse hair. He hitches a little of it to a hook in the centre of a rough wheel and walks slowly away from it.

The wheel turns slowly under the hand of his infant son, who gazes across the sea, dreaming of the ships on which he will never be able to sail; for he, too, belongs to the long generations of Human Spiders who have been working here in the open air for centuries.

As the spinner walks in the sun his fingers play about his cocoon, like the delicate fingers of a violinist on the strings, and there comes from him, miraculously, this line of fine twine, attaching him to the revolving wheel, growing with such speed as he moves away that he seems to be performing the old conjuring trick of producing interminable ribbon from a hat.

He and his ancestors have been spinning here in the open air for more than six hundred years. From here his predecessors saw the dreaded sails on the sky-line, warning them of the approach of Barbary pirates. They saw, too, the galleys of the defeated Moors lurking round the coast, seeking in vain to

81

recapture the island from which Rey Jaime Conquistador had driven them.

We ask him how he spins this thread so miraculously with his fingers. He shrugs his shoulders,
and his dark face smiles at us. He can scarcely
tell ; he scarcely knows himself. He cannot teach
us his craft, any more than a spider can teach a
clumsy beetle how to make a web. It is a craft to
which he was born.

" I knew it," he tells us, " when I was so young
that I could say no more than twenty words, even
before I had much skill in walking. It is simple.
See."

He calls a still smaller son, who comes with the
uncertain steps of early childhood, and, taking a
bundle of the yellow fibre from his father, walks
away from the revolving wheel, frowningly intent
on the cocoon at his waist. His small, fat fingers
are busy in the soft mass, and from it he produces
a twine, as his father had done : a rougher, less
expert twine, but one with which any man might
tether his mule or hang himself. The father
watches, his eyes full of pride for the infant spinner.
He has no worldly goods, no title nor riches to
bestow on his son ; but he has given the boy this

art, and knows that the tradition of the family will be carried on after he has passed.

He is a willing, eager little man. He takes us to a shed and shows us the string he had made, scores of bundles of it wound on sticks. Then, as the Spirit expressed a desire to try her skill at the work, he handed her a cocoon of fibre. He watched her efforts with a kind of bright-eyed sympathy and an eagerness for her success ; when she failed he shook his head regretfully, as though it hurt him to see her fail.

" Had I better tip him ? " I asked as we were leaving.

" I don't know," replied the Spirit. " Perhaps—as we've taken him from his work—and yet he doesn't look a tipable man."

I offered him a peseta, rather reluctantly. He smiled deprecatingly and waved it away. And then I saw a small fat hand appear from behind the wheel, an open hand, palm upwards ! I dropped the peseta into it as I passed. The owner of the hand glanced quickly at the father, but the father had not observed the treachery of the son !

We glanced back before we passed out of sight. The destination of the ill-gotten peseta was revealed to us by a cloud of white dust moving rapidly towards the nearest pastry-cook's shop. Somewhere in the cloud was a boy!

Further along the sea-road we meet the water-seller, taking his cart-load of brimming earthenware jars into the narrow streets. He delivers water daily, like a milkman, selling it for a few centimos a jar to the poor, who have no *patios* in which wells can be sunk. He is lithe and vigorous. He stops at a house, hoists a heavy jar on to each shoulder, and walks majestically with them through a doorway and up a flight of stairs. The carrying of water-pots upon the head or the shoulders might be adopted as a daily exercise for those who aim to improve their carriage ; more than any other form of manual work it develops that dignity and grace of bearing so much sought after by those who have nothing else to recommend them. The act of carrying stiffens the poise of the body, but when the burden is removed the figure falls into a natural and easy grace.

I think this water-seller was a little conscious of his fine bearing, for when he saw the camera that the Spirit was carrying he hesitated, drew himself up to his full stature, glanced tentatively at the camera and smiled. It was an invitation that we could not refuse. He posed like a young god, and when the snap had been taken he extended one of his water jars, offering us a drink.

III.—NEW FRIENDS

TO-DAY we have a visit to pay.

We had heard in Paris of a certain priest who possessed great skill as a musician, and we had been urged to hear him play. " He makes the hair stand upon end," we had been told.

So this afternoon, when the wider streets of Palma are filled with quivering heat, we have come down to the cathedral to search for the priestly musician.

The cathedral is dim and cool after the glare and heat of the streets. It is almost dark. High up at one end is a great circular window of stained glass, through which the sun penetrates in long, slanting searchlight rays of many colours, staining the stone floor, staining us with alternating blue and scarlet, yellow and purple as we passed through them.

The Spirit becomes a character actress : at one moment she was the Scarlet Woman, at another the Yellow Peril. Strange effects these shafts of colour have on human beings in the dimness. One moment a face appears sinister and terrible in yellow, the next ghastly in blue, or horrible with the tint of blood. We had a shock of horror, and the Spirit

87

uttered a little cry, when a gruesome, pale purplish face looked up at us suddenly from the ground. But it was only one of a number of old women washing the floor. They work on hands and knees in a long line across the cathedral, creeping slowly backward; and when a coloured ray rests on their wrinkled faces and shining eyes it changes them into uncanny theatrical witches. The soft slither of their wet cloths over the floor is like the sound of serpents sliding across stone. A producer of Grand Guignol could not obtain a finer effect.

When our eyes were adapted to the dimness we passed round the cathedral and at last found the sacristan in a side-chapel, removing his white legal wig and crimson vestments. He had a fine, thin ascetic face that reminded us of a certain ex-Lord Chancellor. He came out of the Chapel with a serene dignity and told us that Organista Thomas was away, but that he would return later. If we would call at six o'clock in the evening we should see him. He would tell Organista Thomas that we desired to see him, and Organista Thomas would surely await us.

Then he escorted us as we walked. He did not attempt to establish himself as our cicerone; he walked with calm dignity beside us. He seemed to be dreaming. Occasionally he repeated, "Yes, surely he will await you," then he was silent again. His eyes seemed to be searching into some remote distances, calmly and without impatience. Presently we went out into the blinding sunlight and sat on the old wall by the sea to wait for our priestly musician.

He was waiting for us when we returned, standing under the archway on which rested the great organ; and with him was our white-wigged sacristan, who stretched out his hand towards us in a gesture of recognition, and then moved softly and dreamily away. Organista Thomas did not know us; he had never heard of us; but he came towards us with a quick eagerness. One felt the charm of him before one touched his hand. A dark, vivacious little man, with the glowing eyes of an enthusiast. A sensitive face of quick-changing expressions; sudden laughter, and as sudden seriousness. While he talked his hands moved continuously in delicate expressive gestures, and the soft modulations of his voice were music in the dim silence.

He greeted us in French, asking what he could do for us. We replied:

" In Paris we heard of your skill with the organ.

We were told : ' You must hear him play ; it makes the hair rise on the head.' So we have come to hear—and you see, we have not had our hair cut ! "

How he laughed ! The hair on the head ! That was good. Well, now ; certainly he would play for us, if it would give us pleasure, but not now. To-morrow, if we could come, he would play for us ; he would arrange a little programme for, say, an hour—if we could bear an hour of it ! . . . And perhaps we would like to see the piano of Chopin on which the Raindrop prelude was composed ?

The Spirit's eyes nearly popped out of her head, for she has a reverence for such relics. Was the actual piano of Chopin here, in Palma ? Could she see it ?

Yes, he said, it was still here, where the musician left it, in the home of Señora ——. Señora —— was a member of the Canut family, who had induced Chopin to come to Majorca. He would be pleased to take us to Señora —— if we would care to see the piano.

We feared we were encroaching too much on his kindness.

" Ah, no," he said, " we who live in the Isle of Tranquility, away from the world, love well to show

our treasures to the world when the world calls
on us."

We wandered about the cathedral with him while
he talked. Then he led us to the door of a little
winding stone stairway in a side-chapel and took
us up to the organ loft. He hovered about the
keyboard of the organ, explaining the multitudinous
stops and talking of the music he loved best to play.
He had an extraordinary repertoire; every work of
every composer that we mentioned he could play
from memory. Purcell, Stravinski, Goossens, he
knew them all and could play them all.

Presently he said to the Spirit : " Come now,
to-day you shall play to me."

She protested that she had never played an organ,
that the piano was her instrument, but he encouraged her to try.

" I will blow for you," he said, and disappeared
through some cavern among the forest of shining
pipes.

Soon, groanings and creakings and knockings came
from the great organ. The Spirit sat staring at the
long double manual and the multitude of stops like
one fascinated. She raised her hands tentatively and
dropped them nervously. Then she gathered up her

91

courage and placed one hand on the lower keyboard.

A shrill, tootling wail echoed round the cathedral. She snatched her hands away as though the ivories were bars of white-hot fire. A pair of startled eyes looked up at me. She leaned over the parapet and looked down into the depths of the cathedral. Several ghostly faces, horribly coloured by the searchlight from the window, were staring up at the organ ; faces of priests entering to prepare for evensong, startled by that wailing cry !

A voice giving encouragement came through the pipes from the back of the organ, and the Spirit tried again, and this time she had a moderate success. She played " The Poet Speaks," and when she had finished the organ ceased from groaning and peace descended on the cathedral.

Organista Thomas emerged from his forest of pipes. The Spirit's eyes were round with awe as she looked at him. The knowledge that she had been producing harmonious sounds from that great organ almost overcame her !

" But—that terrible wail ! " she said. " It startled all the priests down there."

The little organist moved his hands in delicate deprecation.

92

" No," he said, " they will think it was the voice of an angel ! "

93

He looked terribly serious for a second, his head on one side, and then his eyes gleamed with laughter.

Before we left he had made an appointment for the next morning. He would give his recital at ten o'clock, and after that we should go to see Señora —— and her treasure of a piano. He stood at the cathedral door like a joyous imp, smiling us away.

Truly we were beginning to find the soul of Majorca ; that spirit of joyous service of which we had so many examples later. In how many capitals, I wonder, could one find a cathedral organist who would give a recital to two insignificant strangers whose only introduction was the chance remark of an acquaintance ? . . .

When we appeared in the morning the smiling musician presented us with a little typewritten programme of representative music, which he had prepared specially for us. This is it :

" Gagliarda " . .	*B. Schmid* (16th cent.)
" Pavana Italiana " .	*de Cabezon* (1510–1566)
" Minuetto de la Sona-	*Moreno* (18th century)
tina "	
" Pavana " . . .	*Byrd* (1538–1623)
" Prelude and Fugue .	
in F M." . .	*Bach* (1685–1750)

94

"Offertoire pour la
   Messe. de Minuit" *Franck* (1822–1890)
"Honour alone" .   . *Bach*
"Ronde des Princesses,"
   from "l'Oiseau de
   Feu"   .   .   . *Stravinski* (first style)
"Choral de l'Histoire
   du Soldat" .   . *Stravinski* (last style)

We sat on the far side of the cathedral to get the full
effect of the music.   And then for an hour he played.

If I belonged to the deadly band of musical
critics I should tell you that he played with "charm
and distinction," or that he gave a performance
which was "wholly pleasing," or that his rendering
of Bach's Prelude and Fugue "left nothing to be
desired" : vague generalities of journalism as
meaningless as life. Who can presume adequately
to describe the works of genius interpreted by a
genius ? Not I. It is enough for me to say that
this hour was for us the most emotional hour we had
experienced for a year. Enough to say that we sat
with hushed breath ; that the floor-washing witches
ceased their interminable snake-swishing and sat
back on their shoes while the searchlights painted

their listening faces; that people who wandered into the cathedral stood still, and remained standing there until the music ceased and the last echo whispered itself into silence far up in the invisible roof. . . .

A swish of raiment behind us—" And now," said the little organist, " shall we go to meet the famous piano ? "

We reached the apartment of Señora —— after a short walk through the narrow winding streets in the heart of the city. We found her a pleasant, rather shy woman, with two small curly-haired boys hanging to her skirts and peeping at us from behind her. The walls of the room in which she and her dark, massive husband received us were hung with hundreds of plates of every conceivable size, period, colour and design. It was a National Gallery of plates, of which the family were intensely proud.

Señor —— lifted some of them down for us to examine. He handled them as connoisseurs always handle their treasures : tenderly, almost with awe. Only his politeness prevented him from retaining his hold on them while we examined them ! He was never quite happy while one of his plates was in the hands of a stranger

"The ancient olive"

Lendon mallorca

MAJORCAN OLIVE, 1,000 YEARS OLD

Facing page 96

Chopin's piano stood against the wall of a darkened inner room. We were ushered in with a kind of hushed reverence, and the blinds were raised. The five of us, with the two children still hanging to their mother's skirts, stood round the rosewood piano while the lid was reverently raised from the keyboard.

It was an oddly dwarfed instrument compared with the modern piano, without a full compass of notes. On a kind of gilded antimacassar that was spread along the top of it stood a multitude of small ornaments, statuettes and miniature busts. On the wall behind was a framed letter from Chopin, in which the musician wrote certain instructions concerning the piano. Next to that was a photograph of George Sand and another of Madame Canut. The whole room was a shrine for the pathetic little piano which Chopin brought to Majorca and abandoned.

The Spirit touched a chord: Señora —— and her husband exchanged a glance. The Spirit played with one hand the first few bars of the Prelude: Señora —— and her husband exchanged a look of pain. This piano is not to be played, it is too precious a treasure. So the Spirit refrained, contenting herself with gazing at the instrument.

99

This piano caused Chopin a great deal of trouble and misery, Señora —— told us. He brought it to Palma in 1838 when, on the invitation of her relative, Madame Canut, he arrived with George Sand, his lover, in search of health. The Customs of Palma must have been very much more severe then than now, for they held up the piano. Even though it was the one thing that Chopin needed above all else, they held it up.

Chopin was at first irritated, then distracted. Terrific arguments developed round the harmless instrument. Weeks passed, and still the piano was held up at the Customs headquarters down there by the cathedral. The arguments became so interminable that at last Chopin wished the piano at the bottom of the harbour; but even that was not permitted! At last he managed to secure its release on payment of 400 pesetas, about twenty pounds.

The Spirit asked and obtained permission to photograph the piano, and after more talk and further inspections of household treasures we took leave of the shy wife and her massive husband.

When we were alone the Spirit said : " I simply must play a piano—*must*. I haven't touched a note for a week. All this music—and the spirit of Chopin—makes me savage for the feel of a key-board. Let's go back to the hotel, take the night-gown off the piano and play all the afternoon."

We went back. The piano was locked. We sought the black cat, but he was missing. Then we found a melancholy old woman, who turned out to be his mother, and we asked her for the key. She shook her head.

" No, señora, no, not for a year must music be heard in this home," she said.

We asked her why. She pointed to the photograph of the fat girl over the piano.

" *She* used to play that piano," said the old woman." " Ah, and how she played it ; oh, how she played that piano ! She played it until two days before she died—this child, my son's child."

We understood then the reason for the white shroud and the locked instrument. The girl had died a few months before and, according to local custom, the piano must remain mute.

This knowledge did not cool the Spirit's ardour to make music, though she was bitterly disappointed.

" Never mind, we'll go out and find a shop where you can practise," I consoled her. And out we went. We began the search light-heartedly enough, but presently we became tired and hot in the blaze of the afternoon sun. In London or Paris or Berlin or Madrid we would have found a score of establishments in half an hour, but here it was apparently a hopeless quest. The Spirit became more resolute as she grew more fatigued ; her lips were set firmly and her eyes were filled with an almost fanatical determination ; she was obsessed by a sort of musical nostalgia.

We discovered a shop at last. It combined the sale of pianos and music with the sale of sewing machines. Four girls sat working inside. We entered and asked a swarthy, gross young man, who scowled at us, if he had a piano practice room. No ; he appeared never to have heard of such a thing. But, we persisted, might not the señora play for a little time on one of these pianos ? No, said the young man gloomily, realizing that we were not likely customers, she might not. (I swear from his surly manners that he was a Catalan from Barcelona.)

A pause. Then her eyes rested on a pile of music. There was a wicked gleam in her eyes.

Ah, well, then perhaps we would buy some music, she said. The young man brightened a little and became more attentive (undoubtedly he was a

Catalan from Barcelona !). The Spirit then turned over a few pieces. This, she said, taking up a volume of Beethoven Sonatas priced at 20 pesetas, looked like good music. Could he recommend it ? Oh, yes, the young man could undoubtedly recommend it ; he even recommended a more elaborately bound volume for 35 pesetas. The Spirit gave him one of her most seraphic smiles and asked, might she try one or two of the pieces ? But certainly she might.

She sat at the piano with the sonatas before her. To see her scanning them with a little pucker of the forehead one would never have suspected that she knew them all by heart. She made a tentative, stumbling opening, and then began to play. And how she played ! I could hear all the nostalgia bursting out of her !

I have no record of how long she played, but it was so long that the young man became restless. At the end of the third sonata the Spirit shook her head. No, she didn't care for those pieces. Had he anything else, anything a little better ?

He produced " Chopin's Preludes and Nocturnes," very elaborate, gold-embossed, 42 pesetas. Yes, that looked good, she said, and then she sat down and gave me the most perfect ten minutes of Chopin.

103

The young man became suspicious. The sounds of suppressed giggles came from the four girls who bent over their work. The young man scowled and strode into his office, from the window of which I could see his face glowering at us.

By this time the Spirit had run away from her music and was playing anything that came into her head. She was having an orgy of emotional expression, she was wallowing in music.

Presently the young man came out again, black as a thunder-cloud. The Spirit smiled sweetly at him. Had he anything just a little better, something. . . .

No, he had not, most definitely he had not—nothing at all, nothing !

Then perhaps, said the Spirit, taking up a single copy of a Spanish song marked 2 pesetas, she would just take this. She paid her two pesetas with another seraphic smile at the young man. He scowled us out of the shop. He will never forgive us, nor his four work-girls for joining on our side against him, nor life for creating him as it did, nor his patron saint for allowing him to be beaten. But I hope it taught him a lesson for his incivility. Certainly the Spirit's music-hunger had been satisfied, for she went back to dinner effervescing like soda water.

On the way back I discovered in a side street a potter's shop in which some attractive pottery was displayed. We examined it through the doorway, and some of the articles attracted the Spirit. There were fine red-clay water pots, shaped in the Greek style ; there were peasant plates and vases done in crude simple colourings ; but best of all was a flat, rounded pot of blue and white, narrowing away at the top and then opening out in a broad curving mouth. It had a simple grace that delighted us. We bought it.

" It will look wonderful," said the Spirit, " with red carnations in it."

When we reached our room at the hotel the swarthy maid was prodding the pipe of the wash-bowl with her hairpin, trying to get rid of the morning washing water. She watched the Spirit deposit her vase on a table.

" Muy bella," purred the Spirit, standing back and regarding her find.

" Ah, si, muy bella," said the woman. " Muy bella escupidor."

" Muy bella *what* ? " asked the Spirit.

" She says," I interposed, " that it's a very beautiful spitoon."

" Good heavens ! "

Pause.

" Si, si, bella escupidor, verimente," said the woman.

Pause.

" Well, anyhow, it's beautiful," said the Spirit. " Spitoon or not, I'm going to have red carnations in it." (And to this day she has, and nobody is any the wiser !)

106

IV.—THE VILLAGE OF THE LILIES.

IT is time for us to take a temporary leave of Palma. We are going to Valldemosa, the first village in the hills, the village of Chopin.

We intend to explore the whole of the mountainous north of the island to the east coast, and we are going into districts where there are no railways. The wanderer must devise his own mode of travel. He may go by mule, or in a covered cart—except in the mountains—or by bumping, rattling motor diligence, or on his feet.

As we did not wish to be encumbered with luggage, we searched Palma for a knapsack. But Palma had no knapsacks—she had plenty of wicker baskets, to be balanced on the head, but it seemed absurd to carry one's tooth brush and razor in a basket on one's head. The difficulty solved itself, however, when we noticed the Spirit's umbrella and sunshade case lying in a corner of our room.

The very thing, we decided. Leave the umbrellas with our luggage in charge of the hotel, push our small necessities down the umbrella case—like filling a Christmas stocking—and sling it across

my back like a rifle. We experimented and found
the idea admirable. It gave me a martial appearance,
but when the Spirit began to drill me and I obeyed
her order to " slope arms," the gun discharged a
tooth-brush and a pyjama coat.

We found that we could make the first stage of the
journey as far as Valldemosa by motor diligence.
These are the vehicles of the poor. You may travel
miles and miles for a peseta ; our fare to Valldemosa
cost us about sevenpence for twelve miles. But
when we reached the square that was the place of
departure of the daily diligence we found that it had
already gone, half an hour before scheduled time.

The proprietor of the diligence, who keeps a café
in the square, explained it all by the one word
fiesta. The frequent *fiestas* thoroughly disorganize
Majorcan life. Crowds of peasants come into the
capital ; the diligences forget their scheduled times ;
and all the food in the cafés and restaurants is eaten
up long before evening.

But, said the diligence owner, we need have no
fear. We should go to Valldemosa. The diligence
had gone because it was full ; well, he would find
another diligence. There were a dozen people
besides ourselves who wanted to get to Valldemosa.

He did not find another diligence, but somehow, from somewhere, he found a large touring car. This, we said to ourselves, was going to cost us much money, but when we asked for tickets the fare was still one peseta, even though we were to travel in state in a large touring car.

Now the average large car is seldom built to carry more than seven or eight persons, including the driver. This car carried fourteen. I cannot tell you where they were all accommodated. I know there was a man cradled somewhere in the folds of the lowered hood at the back, because his foot was in perpetual contact with my ear. I know there was a shawled peasant girl sitting on my right knee and lying back on my shoulder, because I could smell the garlic in her breath. I know there were two lively young male peasants folded up on each footboard, because clouds of asphyxiating smoke from four *fiesta* cigars continually swirled over the sides of the car into our faces. And I know that when all our limbs had been somehow fitted into this human jig-saw, when our heads, like the heads of swimmers, came to the surface of this pool of humanity for air, I heard a muffled plaintive voice from somewhere saying :

" Isn't it jolly—going native ! . . ."

The road to Valldemosa begins as a straight, dusty, dull way that would have filled the heart of William Cobbett with satisfaction, for it is a pathway through the Gardens of Utility. Through corn-fields it goes, through groves of misted-green olive trees distorted into the harsh shapes of old age. Every inch of plain outside the city is cultivated.

Lean, bronzed peasants bend their backs over the rich red earth or take their siesta under the olives. The road is deserted except for an occasional cart drawn by a donkey or a swift-trotting horse.

But after a few miles we reached the bases of the hills and began to mount through tumbled grey rocks, through ravines and along roads cut in the side of the mountain. The car is travelling at forty miles an hour. It takes a corner with a sickening swerve and carries us along a shelf above a splashing torrent. One twitch of the steering wheel and we should be through the rough stone parapet, bounding and rolling down to the torrent. Goats and sheep browse among the grey rocks; sometimes they scatter as we swirl past, and we hear faintly the music of their bells.

Another corner that brings a catch to the breath. How he drives, this lean young hillman! He is so sure of himself. The last stage of the journey takes us up a terrifying road like a great spiral staircase. Corner after corner we skirl round in swift, graceful semi-circles.

The four footboard passengers are grim and silent; they have thrown away their cigars and are holding on for their lives. The unseen but acutely felt presence wrapped in the hood is tossed about as the car bounds over ruts, and every rut adds a bruise to my ear. The peasant girl has never travelled in this manner, she knows only the slower, safer diligence. She is pale, her lips are set, and her breath comes and goes quickly in my immune ear.

Suddenly we swing out of the spiral and into Valldemosa. The daily arrival and departure of the diligence is an event in Valldemosa. Full-bosomed interested women come to their wide-arched doorways to see us pass. The village is like the Himalayan kingdom in which Namgay Doola caused so great a disturbance : most of it stands on end. The streets of small grey houses, rough-built of mountain rock, rise steep to the monastery and the church that dominate the village.

The car stops with a screech of brakes outside the village *fonda*, and after a sorting out of legs and arms and personal belongings, we alight. We are greeted by a bearded, beaming fat woman. It is no pretence of a beard that she has, but a real black curling affair that hides all her chin. Her eyes are the true Majorcan eyes : big, luminous, and glowing with friendliness.

" Buenas, Señor, buenas, Señora."

At once one feels at home here. One feels almost mothered. The bearded one gathers us in rather than leads us—through the café bar of the inn, where the men of the village are sitting over their innocuous drinks, filling the bare white room with the cataract of talk that you hear whenever two or more Majorcans are gathered together. Nods and smiles as we pass, and the mutter of " *Buenas* "—the abbreviated greeting that they always give us. It is never *buenas dias*—good day—but simply *Buenas*—Good ; perhaps the best expression of their feelings, for they wish you nothing but the best in life.

Upstairs we find ourselves in a clean whitewashed room with a floor of red tiles and two small white beds, a tin washstand, wooden pegs behind the door, but no cupboards. Seldom do you find a cupboard in a Majorcan bedroom. Its absence is a comment on the simplicity of life of these island people, for why should they have cupboards when they possess no wardrobe ? An extra skirt perhaps, and a special white shawl for *fiesta* days—that is the most a Majorcan woman needs for her adornment. As for shoes, an additional pair of *spadanias*, the string-soled, heelless footwear with buff or brown canvas uppers, is enough for any wife or maid.

113

The entire absence of competition in dress is one of the small secrets of the happiness of these women, the Spirit says. Teresa here is not whipped into envy because Juliana, her neighbour, excels her in personal adornment, for Juliana and Teresa wear twin clothes. Juliana cannot stand at her door and make cutting comments, born of jealousy, to her husband on the bad taste or vulgarity of Teresa's new creation. They are uniformed, every one of them, hence they have little interest in each other's garments.

The bearded one came in with a pile of snowy linen, every piece of which had her monogram embroidered in a corner. We left her making our beds and went out, down the steep street of the village. At once we found a name for Valldemosa. It is the Village of the Lilies. At almost every wide doorway there is a pot wherein grows a graceful white lily. All down one side of the narrow street you will see these flowers, tended with exquisite care. So universal was this lily that at first we thought it had some special significance, but when we inquired later, we were told that it was *la habitud*—just the custom. The lily is the aspidistra of Valldemosa. Its buds are counted and encouraged daily, as the sprouting leaves of the weary suburban aspidistra on its bamboo tripod are counted and encouraged by the English housewife.

Few of the houses of Valldemosa have windows downstairs; they have instead an arched doorway wide enough to pass a cart. The heavy oak door is always thrown wide open, and as we pass we see the interiors. The floors are stone-paved, the walls of purest white unadorned; each entrance has the appearance of a castle hall in miniature. The two sides of this white hall are lined with rows of little low oak chairs, perhaps six on each side, perhaps more. The seats of these are made of the string which our Human Spider and his confrères have spun. It is woven across the chairs in a criss-cross design, layer upon layer of string, making a strong, comfortable seat.

These chairs are the fetish of the Majorcan wife; she who has not at least four on each side of her hall cannot call her house a respectable home. Yet her chairs are more than mere conventional furnishings; they are also the symbol of Majorcan hospitality. They are an invitation and a promise, as we soon discovered.

We had paused in front of one of these peasant castles when the string curtain that hung over the doorway parted and a woman looked out at us. She smiled, and invited us to enter. When we were inside she gestured towards the chairs and invited us to sit, whereupon she went to the arched doorway at the other end of the hall and called out in the patois.

There was a scamper of feet and four girls came in. Three of them were brown-skinned, vigorous young women with bright, laughing eyes ; the fourth was a hunchback whose white face was full of a soft shy radiance. After they had greeted us they sat with the mother on the row of chairs on the opposite side, and the conversation was conducted across the hall.

They spoke Spanish in addition to their own patois. They asked us about London. Was it a very big city, bigger than Palma ? Yes, it was fifty, a hundred times as big as Palma. (They could hardly believe that). Was it true that there was always rain and never sunshine there ? And the English language—was it very difficult ? Would we teach them some words of English ?

Our efforts to teach them to pronounce " Good morning " were interrupted by the arrival of the master of the home : a shy but friendly man of the hills, bronzed, blue eyed, and lean like all the

Majorcans. After he had greeted us he went to the kitchen, which was separated from the hall by a stone partition three feet high, looked into a pan that was standing on the charcoal fire, and brought it across to show us the contents, with an invitation that we should share it. We thanked him and declined, remembering the tragedy of the bread and honey. A refusal does not hurt their feelings, for they expect it ; their offer of food is only the expression of their friendliness.

When we parted the family gathered in the stone doorway to see us off, and as soon as the string curtain had fallen into place the sound of an excited babble of voices followed us up the narrow street. Our visit had given them material for discussion for a week.

We ate that night in the most exquisite dining-room that ever graced a country inn. Imagine a pure white room, small enough to be intimate, bare-walled and dustless ; a red-tiled floor ; three green-shuttered windows ; four white tables, each bearing an unglazed water-pot of Greek design, filled with large crimson roses. Imagine a plump, brown-faced, smiling girl softly padding about in her string *spadanias*, producing bottles of red wine from under her shawl like a conjurer. Imagine her—especially when you are hungry—bringing you steaming hot vegetable soup, a dish piled with lamb chops, fresh green vegetables, artichokes, beans, fried cabbage ; then a mountain of oranges, fresh purple figs, red cherries and yellow nespolis. We finished one bottle of wine and another appeared from under the magic shawl ; then a syphon of soda-water to mix with the wine. The island innkeepers stint us of nothing, yet they charge us no more than seven pesetas, or four and sixpence a day ; and for a long stay they will reduce the daily charge to five or six pesetas. These prices are almost universal in the island.

There were only three other guests at the inn : a German, his wife, and a tall young Austrian. They told us that they were Chopin worshippers on pilgrimage to the monastery. Had we, too, come to see the monastery ? Yes, we were going there to-morrow. This established a bond of common interest, and we talked for an hour of music, and Majorca, and life, and the good-heartedness of the bearded innkeeper.

When we went up to the cool white bedroom the night sounds of Valldemosa rose through the open windows ; soft sounds as full of music as the name

of the village. The tolling of the monastery bell ;
the faint and far away jingle of sheep-bells, and more
than all else the crooning, human voice of the wind,
rising and falling, whispering, crying out in pain, or
laughing a soft, maniacal laugh. All night the wind
makes weird and perpetual harmony that seems
like the voice of nature brooding over one of her
fairest gems. Far off in the valley a nightingale
sings ; then two, three nightingales. Somewhere,
muted by walls, there is the twang of a guitar.

Who can doubt that Chopin found inspiration in
this village of music ? He came here seeking peace
and the warmth of the winter sun. He arrived in
the winter of 1838, when he was 28 years of age and
his companion, George Sand, was 34. The musician
was ill, consumptive ; and Maurice, the son of
George Sand, was almost an invalid. The party
arrived in Majorca after a terrible journey from
Barcelona in a pig boat, for there was then no
service of passenger boats to the islands.

They did not come immediately to Valldemosa.
At first they rented a small house near their friends
in Palma, but this they were soon forced to quit by
a landlord who had no sympathy with consumptives.
George Sand then learned that one of the cells in

the monastery was available for a rental of 35
pesetas a year, and this opportunity was too good
to be missed. After a journey up into the hills,
during which, according to George Sand, one wheel
of the cart that carried them was on the mountain
and the other in the ravine, they installed themselves in the monastery.

La Cartuja stands on the hill at the end of a deep
valley that winds away through the hills, through
the grey rocks and the misted olive groves, until it
reaches Palma by the sea. Before the monastery
became the home of Carthusian monks it was the
palace of kings. Musa the Moor first made it his
pleasure garden, before Rey Jaime Conquistador
overthrew the eastern power and gave Majorca back
to herself. Then Sancho the Asthmatical built his
palace on the site in 1321, but, fearing death, he
built so hurriedly that nothing of his work survives.
Other kings followed him there, until at last Martin
the Pious, living up to his name, presented the site
to the Carthusians in 1399. The monks built cells
and cloisters for solitary meditation. " A small
house of four rooms with a garden, each cell opening into one corridor "—those were the rules of the
order ; and it was one of these " small houses "

that the ailing Chopin occupied with George Sand and her two children, three years after the monks had been ejected by the Spanish Government and the monastery turned into apartments.

When we climbed the hill in the morning and walked round the building we could find no entry. The doors of the church were locked. Presently a swarthy, solemn man appeared at the doorway of a house and, after asking us if we wished to enter, produced a small boy, telling him to fetch the sacristan.

Ten minutes later a strange and terrible creature, scarcely human in form, jerked its way up the hill towards us. His legs were bent in towards the right, like twin bows. His body was half doubled, so that he moved in a crouching attitude. His arms and long bony fingers twitched in horrible spasmodic jerks. He slobbered at the mouth, and a little wailing moan escaped him as he walked. A bunch of keys dangled from one hand, and when he reached us he spoke in the patois in a thick, whining voice. His deformities filled us with pain. He was so terrible a figure that the Spirit had to turn her face away.

He shambled and jerked his way past us and with a twitching hand unlocked the door of the church and led us in. But we were not interested in the church, and at last we made him understand what we wished to see. With dragging, painful steps that still forced from him that wailing moan he took us through a door at the back of the church into a long white corridor.

This corridor is fourteen feet wide and five hundred feet long. It is the longest, whitest corridor I have ever seen. On one side the windows look on to the cloistered garden; on the other the whiteness is broken at intervals by small green doors. These are the monastery apartments, now occupied by Majorcan families.

The deformed sacristan jerked himself forward and rattled his keys against the second door. It was opened after a brief delay by a short, mild-eyed man.

Was this the apartment of Chopin? we asked.

Yes; would we care to view it? We entered a low white room with a beamed ceiling and French windows at the far end. We were first attracted by two small landscape paintings on the wall, which proved on examination to be the work of Sargent. We expressed surprise at finding them here in this island monastery, and asked the little man where he had found them. He told us he bought them in

Madrid, and that he was a Majorcan artist, which seemed to be sufficient explanation. Then he took us round the apartment, showing us his treasures, his tapestries, his Majorcan linens.

In the dining-room he had a fine carved Spanish table covered with blue and white *tela de lengua*, the ancient woven linen, vegetable-dyed. Round the room were arranged the inevitable chairs of hospitality, quaint, straight-backed, simple string-seated shairs. There were no pictures here, only plates of blue and white and bright yellow. String matting covered the floor.

Presently he led us out into the garden. It is small and square, not more than thirty feet across, bounded on one side by the house, on two sides by high walls, and at the end by a low parapet on the edge of a mountain slope so steep that it is almost a precipice. Below, away and away into the haze of heat, meanders the valley with its scattered grey rocks and its olive groves. The sun is hot in this sheltered end of the valley, but a breeze rises from the distant sea, scatters the petals of the roses, and stirs the orange and lemon trees in the garden, so that their golden fruits dip and rise and sway in a perpetual dance.

They should have been happy here, those lovers, the musician and the writer, yet they were not. Partly this was the fault of George Sand. She was an emancipated woman, and made no effort to conceal her emancipation from the simple people of Valldemosa. She shocked them by her actions, by wearing trousers and by smoking in public. She so antagonized these people, to whom Feminism was and is still a mystery, and to whom her religion was a strange Paganism, that they resented her presence in their tranquil village.

If George Sand had made these people her friends instead of her enemies, she and Chopin might have avoided many of the discomforts that beset them. But George Sand was scornful of the narrowness of the Valldemosans; she spoke of them bitterly because they could not understand her and, misunderstanding, disliked her. " Heartless, selfish and impertinent " were the mildest of her adjectives. The Valldemosans withdrew the friendly assistance which they would otherwise have extended to the newcomers, and the visitors were left to fend for themselves.

The winter was cold. They had no fire, though now a wide open hearth has been built in the apartment. Then they had only a charcoal brazier, beside which the invalid Chopin, unhappy and at times querulous, used to sit muffled in top-coats and rugs.

The creation of the Prelude marked the climax of Chopin's miseries in Valldemosa, for soon afterwards the musician and his mistress left Majorca for ever, leaving behind them the pathetic piano on which the Prelude was composed.

The little Majorcan artist is very proud of his apartment. He lives there alone with a housekeeper, his palette, his brushes, his oils, and a piano. When he does not paint he sits in his garden and dreams, and when he tires of dreaming he turns to his piano, so that the beauties of Chopin may still be heard in the room where they were born nearly a century ago.

We took our leave at last, and after a lunch at the *fonda* that would have sufficed for a party of six hungry people, we went down the village to buy certain necessities for our passage through the mountains. Most of all we needed soft shoes, for earlier experiences had taught us the folly of scrambling up ravines and over rocky tracks in leather footwear. The feet swell with the heat of the rocks, the leather compresses the flesh, and walking becomes a mediæval torture. We therefore decided to buy ourselves each a pair of *spadanias*, which are soft and easy for the feet.

The first difficulty that a stranger encounters on a shopping expedition in a Majorcan village is the absence not only of shop signs but of shop fronts. A shop is in no way differentiated from a dwelling house. The shopkeeper does not announce himself boldly with an inscription over his door ; he does not deface his old stone house with " Pedro Estaras, shoe-maker. Orders executed with the utmost promptitude." Everybody knows where he lives, so why should he announce it ? And as for advertising his promptitude, why, that would most distinctly condemn him and create suspicion, for nobody in a Majorcan village is ever prompt, and speed is not an indication of quality in the work of a man who is still an artist, unspoiled by the incursion of modern machinery.

We therefore had to hunt for the shop of Pedro Estaras. We had to pass along the narrow streets and peer and pry through doorways into the private lives of the Valldemosans, until after half an hour we found our little shoemaker at work among his shoes. His shop was crowded with other wares as

well as shoes; with rope and oil, wine in great flagons
and casks, with dried fish, straw hats and baskets.
We sat on a cask of wine while his daughter produced shoes and tried them on our feet, and when we
had made our choice Pedro courteously brought for-

ward three glasses of wine. The shoes cost us six
pesetas—four pesetas for mine and two for the
Spirit's. Two pairs of hand-made shoes with woven
string soles for three shillings and sixpence! One
can afford to walk long distances in Majorca.

127

We set off the next day to walk to Miramar *en route* for Soller, where we would have to hire mules to carry us through the mountains to Pollensa.

In the street we were surprised to see groups of shawled women strolling about with stools under their arms. They were going to church, for it was Sunday morning. In the Majorcan villages the women take their own seats to church with them. You see them flocking up the streets, each with a little string or canvas-seated stool under her arm instead of a prayer-book. Sometimes groups of friends encounter each other, and then there is a general depositing of stools in the street while the friends stand to gossip. But never will they sit on these stools in the street, for that would surely be a slight to the church.

We picked our way through the groups and struck off up the road that leads further into the hills. The bearded old woman who had been our hostess stood to bid us farewell on the doorstep of the *fonda*, with her servant, and her son, and her ass (she had no ox), which was tethered to the wall, and nearly all that was hers. As we turned the corner the last sight we had of Valldemosa was of her smiling face and nodding head.

Our road passed close to a gorge that holds memories of one of Valldemosa's most heroic fights for her women in the stormy days of the past. One night, nearly four hundred years ago, a band of five hundred Barbary pirates, fierce and rapacious men, landed secretly on the coast and crept through the mountains into the village. They sacked the peaceful homes ; the streets ran with the blood of the men of Valldemosa ; and when the pirates swept back towards the coast they took with them for their pleasure several hundred despairing, terrified women and girls.

But the remnants of the men of Valldemosa were gathered together ; fewer than fifty men there were ; yet they pursued the five hundred pirates and trapped them in the gorge. They divided into two parties, advanced from each end of the gorge, and attacked as fiercely as men will who are fighting for their women. The two parties steadily cut their way through the pirates until they met over the bodies of their enemies, and by morning the wives and daughters were back in their homes in Valldemosa.

There are other epics of Valldemosa, but that is the noblest. Valldemosa surely has earned her peace and deserves her nightingales.

V.—PIGS IN PARADISE

THE road to Miramar winds round the mountain side through pines and olive groves until it reaches the soft azure sea. But before we came to the sea we cut across a rocky slope through a wilderness of Spanish oaks that grew among the grey crags and boulders.

We were passing through the cool green gloom in the silence when we heard a rustling in the undergrowth. The sound came from all directions and seemed to be converging upon us. A few minutes later a score of black snouts protruded through the surrounding bushes, and as we passed the owners of the snouts emerged and began to follow us.

Now it is disconcerting to be followed through a forest by an army of lean black pigs. Normal fat pigs on a farmyard are harmless enough, but lean pigs that run in the forest with the speed of dogs and follow at a distance convey an unpleasantly sinister threat. We looked for tusks, but they did not appear to possess these dangerous appendages.

We shoo-ed them; they stopped, peering silently at us from under the long flapping ears that hung over their eyes. Not a grunt came from them to prove that they were normal healthy pigs. We went on, and they continued to follow, pattering along, stopping when we stopped and making a

pretence of foraging among the rocks for food. It was only pretence, because as soon as we walked on they ceased their foraging and pattered untiringly behind us again. Presently we saw more lean

black pigs running towards us from the direction
in which we were going.

" I don't like it," said the Spirit, whose nerves
were becoming frayed by this silent, relentless
shadowing. " They're trying to wear us down.
Some day someone will find our bleached bones
under a tree. I will not be eaten by wild pigs.
We must *do* something."

I threw a stone ; the pigs scattered, only to close
in again. Others came trotting through the trees,
sensing us in some mysterious way, and joined the
group until there were nearly forty of the beasts.
Pigs were closing in on us from every point of the
compass. It was like a black and horrible army
gathering for attack. We tried to shake them off
by running, but they also ran, and they were more
accustomed than we to scrambling over rocky ground.

Never in any circumstances put yourself in a
position that permits you to be followed by an army
of lean, black, silent pigs. That way madness lies.
You are defenceless, you are alone in the silent
forest ; your every movement is watched by forty
pairs of gleaming eyes until your nerves fray to shreds.

Presently the Spirit gave a cry of relief and sped
ahead of me. We had reached a four-foot wall built

133

of unmortared stones, and beyond it the road showed white in the burning sun. We reached the wall, climbed over, and turned to triumph over the pigs.

The pigs stood a moment staring back at us over the wall. Then with one accord they turned to the right and ran along beside the wall until they disappeared. This unaccountable behaviour mystified us until suddenly we saw, far up the road, a lean black pig appear through a hole in the wall. Another and another followed.

" Oh, God ! " cried the Spirit, and began to run.

One has heard that people afflicted with insomnia try to woo sleep by counting imaginary sheep emerging through a hole in a hedge. This may be effective; I do not know. But I know that the sight of forty black pigs emerging one by one through a wall, after they have followed you in silence for miles through the mountain woods, is the figment of a nightmare.

The pursuit was becoming unbearable when a sudden, high-pitched cry sounded from the rocky ground that sloped down to the sea.

" Arr-r-ree-e-e."

The onrush of the herd was abruptly checked. Black snouts, shining moistly in the sunlight, twitched nervously. Then, amazingly, the whole

134

herd turned and fled, not down the mountain into the
sea, after the manner of certain of their ancestors that
were possessed of an evil spirit, but down the road
and back through the wall. One by one they went
through the hole, with their absurd tails waving and
curling behind them, with squeals and grunts of fear.

A Majorcan, lean as the pigs, stood laughing at us
from the olive grove where he had been working.

" That is good," I said. " They have followed us
for many kilometres. They are horrible beasts."

" Ai," he said. " But the señor should have
pulled some nuts from the *alcenas* and thrown to
them. It is all they desired, those beasts."

He told us that they ran free in the mountain
estates, waiting for the fall of the acorns with which
they innocently fatten themselves in readiness for
the slaughterer's knife. We realized that we had
perhaps misjudged the pigs, suspecting them of
sinister intentions when they were merely begging
for acorns ; but even the prospect of acorns does
not excuse such relentless bad manners.

We were now able to give more attention to the
country. And what country it is along that white
coast road that runs a thousand feet and higher along
the mountains above the Mediterranean ! Gazing

down the steep, rock-strewn slopes, across the red soil and the silvery olives to the deep blue of a sea so far below that its wash sounds faintly, like the softest breeze whispering in the pines, one dreads the inevitable day when the passing of some Lord Brougham will change the coast into a place of villas and casinos, of elaborate hotels and fashionable clothes, of sophistication and criminals.

For the natural beauty here is greater than any beauty that the south of France could have offered before it was taken in hand by man, and turned into an artificial paradise. No pretentiousness is here, no artificial magnificence, only the magnificence of nature, whose silver-grey peaks tower above, whose red earth and shining streams go down to the white-ruffled sea. Here they have no more than forty rainy days in the year, and half the days of the winter are cloudless.

And everywhere around us, now that we are progressing further from Palma, the primitive simplicity of the Majorcan countryman's work on the land begins to show itself. He is always an artist, and everywhere you may see the creations of his hands, even in the hinges on which swing the rough wooden gates that divide the cultivated terraces on

"The Spinner"

THE SPINNER OF WOOL

Facing page 136

the mountain slopes.   He does not use iron to hold
the gates in their position, iron that creaks and
streaks the sun-bleached wood with the brown stain
of rust, but carves his hinges from the solid boughs
of the mountain pine or oak.

First the wood is planed to a thickness of two or
three inches, then cut into a crude form that is best
described by comparing it with the shape of a ping-
pong bat.   In the centre of the circular part of the
bat a hole is carved, three inches in diameter.   Even
in this hole the work of the artist shows itself, for
the very edges are smoothed away and rounded to
soften their hardness of line.

Then the handle of the bat is thrust into a hole
in a rock or a wall and held fast by cement, or by a
wedge of wood driven into the stone until the
handle is gripped as by a vice.   Through the circular
hole in this bat one round projecting stave of the
gate is inserted, and the gate swings freely in its
socket of wood.

A simple, primitive, inexpensive hinge ; yet how
much more effective, more permanent and more
beautiful than all the iron and steel creations that have
been wrought by the labour of multitudes of men in
a factory.   These hinges last a lifetime ; they are fool-

proof, rust-proof, personal creations, beautiful in their simplicity. They have the stamp of individuality, and you feel that they have given as much pleasure to their creators as they give to you, the beholder.

The same simple craftsmanship you will see in the irrigation methods. Here and there down the slopes runs a tiny rounded channel, two inches deep and four wide, carrying a runnel of water that shines down the mountain in the sun like a silver thread. For miles some of these handmade streams run down the crags to reservoirs in the vineyards and the olive groves. If you find a pleasure in the simple things that show the work of man's hand, these minute channels, roughly made of cement, will delight you more than all the majesty and strength of a Roman aqueduct. They carry the cool, life-giving water of the mountain springs down the rocky slopes, in humble service, without pomp and circumstance. They are symbols of the character of Majorca, as the mighty aqueducts were symbols of the character of Rome.

Towards sunset we began to look for the inn where we expected to stay that night. It had an interesting history. Many years ago a lonely, love-lorn Austrian Archduke, Ludwig Salvator, came here to find consolation in solitude, bought many miles of mountain and coast, built him a house, and out of the kindness of his heart started a *hospideria* for wayfarers. Here the weary and footsore could find free lodging for three nights, with free linen, olives, salt, and charcoal for their fires. Here we proposed to stay for the night, though not as the guests of the Archduke, for since his death in 1915 the *hospideria*, while still retaining its character, has become a *fonda*.

Presently we met an elderly and unshapely Spanish woman, with an elderly and shapeless girl about twenty years of age. She was picking flowers and grasses from the roadside. We asked her if she could direct us to the *hospideria*.

La hospideria? But we had passed it. Truly we had passed it. Did we not see it, along the road there to the left? Yes, we saw that house, but were under the impression that it was private. No, no, that was the *hospideria*, along to the right. She repeated the direction at least ten times, with vigorous speech and terrific gesture. In spite of our thanks, she persisted in explaining again; the more we thanked her the more she explained. And after five minutes of repeated explanation, when at last we managed to excuse ourselves, she told us that she was staying there herself and would come with us.

All the way back she never ceased from explaining how we had passed the *hospideria*. She explained it five times, with growing excitement, to the proprietor of the *hospideria ;* and all that evening she explained it to the other wayfarers, telling them how she had saved us from going on for ever and ever and never finding the *hospideria*. She felt that she had become the heroine of the moment. By this time we were a little fatigued by hearing how we had passed the *hospideria* on the left.

The old guest-house was a clean, cool place, with the usual bare white walls and tiled floors. The main room was the hall, with a floor of uneven stone paving and wooden benches round the walls. We were given a large bedroom which could be approached only through another large bedroom, which appeared to be unoccupied.

The proprietor, a heavy, pouchy fellow with a big yellowish face, cooked the meals himself over a charcoal stove in a small room opening into the main hall, and his wife and two pretty daughters served the food. The wife was a little woman, with bright brown eyes and quick movements that reminded us of a mouse.

We ate not so well that night, for the food, although plentiful, was coarse. The man was no cook; he soaked everything in gravy and flavoured it with garlic. But this suited the other guests, of whom there were half a dozen, including our elderly shapeless saviour and her daughter. The daughter ate in a kind of sheepish silence, but the mother consumed large mouthfuls while she explained how we had gone past the *hospideria*. Of the other way-farers, one was an enormously rotund woman with a thin husband; then there was a little nondescript man who talked incessantly about business, and a quiet, lame countryman who did not speak at all.

After dinner, when we sat talking on one of the benches against the wall, several doves fluttered through the open door out of the dusk and strutted unheeded about the floor. A lean hound followed, seating himself on the floor and watching the birds with unblinking eyes. The Spaniards were talking incessantly when suddenly, out of the babble of tongues, came a voice from the quiet lame country-man, who for some time had been shyly watching us.

" You gonna stay right here to-night, sir ? " he said.

The accent was the broadest product of America. He explained that he had been ten years in various

143

towns in America, where he had made his little fortune by selling " hot dog " and kindred delicacies ; now he had returned to live at ease in his native land. I said I had no idea that there was so much money in hot dog.

" Sure, dere's money in everything over dere," he said.

He was very proud of having travelled so far to make his fortune, and very pleased to be able to talk a language which was incomprehensible to the other people in the room. I asked him if many Majorcans went to America, but he said no, most of them were content with their own island. I reminded him that it was a Majorcan monk, Junipero Serra, of the Franciscan order, who founded the American city of San Francisco, and he replied :

" He sure was a wise guy—yes, sir."

One sensed a curious conflict of pride in this little Americanized Majorcan. He was proud of having been in America, extolling it as the greatest country in the world ; yet the pride in his native island was greater. He loved us to love Majorca, but he did not care whether we liked or loathed America.

When we were ready for bed the proprietor's wife handed us a candle through a kind of porthole that communicated with the kitchen and we went up the narrow stairs to our room. Unthinkingly we entered the outer chamber that gave access to our own. It was unfortunate, for the outer room was occupied by the rotund Spanish woman and her thin husband.

The unexpected vision of a rotund lady in her under-garments is embarrassing in any circumstances. But when the said vision gives a shrill

squeal, lumbers across the room and crouches behind the bed with only her head showing above it; when her thin husband, wearing a long grey

145

nightgown, rushes round to give her further protection from our gaze—then the situation becomes strained.

We withdrew. We stood outside the door debating what one should do in such a delicate situation. A moment later the door opened and the husband, smiling wanly, apologized for the mishap and invited us to pass through, as the señora was now in bed. We accepted the invitation, taking care to keep our faces well averted from the bed; but I could not resist one glance askance as I entered our own room. The rotund lady, instead of being prostrate with outraged modesty, was sitting up in bed, smiling and nodding us good-night.

We exercised great care the next morning to prevent a repetition of the mishap. We deliberately made a noise in dressing; we scraped a chair on the floor and coughed loudly and repeatedly to give due warning; we knocked twice on our door before opening it to pass out. No reply. When I peered into the next room the pair were lying fast asleep, and the thin husband's arm was thrown protectively across the rotund lady's shoulders. We crept through on tiptoe and so escaped.

Downstairs we had coffee, sour bread, and a

basket of fruit, and after we had paid our bill—
fourteen pesetas, or about nine shillings for the two
of us—we started off again. We intended to visit
the house of the love-lorn Archduke, which we were
told could be viewed ; it was now unoccupied, preserved by its present owner in the state in which
the Archduke left it.

We found the house, a plain, Moorish-looking
structure with two huge palm trees standing in front
of it, on a small plateau, some hundreds of yards
down the mountain-side below the road. The
windows were shuttered, and we approached the
arched doorway and looked into the hall. It
resembled the rest of the Majorcan homes : white
walled, stone-floored, but with two fine archways
at the far end. At one side there was a great oak
trestle table, and behind it, on a bench against the
wall, sat one of the oldest-looking women we had
ever seen.

Her body was bent and her brown face a mass of
deep furrows. She struggled to her feet with the
aid of two sticks. We addressed her in Spanish,
but she knew only Majorcan, which she spoke in a
thin, uncertain, high-pitched voice. She raised one
of her sticks and I thought she was about to strike

147

us ; instead, she brought it down with a crash on the table. Then, muttering to herself, she shuffled over to one of the archways and disappeared in the gloom beyond. We could hear uncanny chuckling noises from the obscurity ; then her dragging foot-steps died away and there was silence.

This was mystifying. We waited a few minutes, but as she did not reappear we began to explore. We had not gone far before footsteps sounded in the hall, and a younger woman appeared, lean, swarthy, and with a black handkerchief tied over her head. She said her mother had told her that we were here, and she had come to show us round. We learned that these two had for many years been servants of the Archduke, and were now the caretakers of the empty house.

She led us upstairs to a big chamber which appears to have been the Archduke's study or sitting-room. It contained some fine carved Spanish chairs, cushioned with blue and white Majorcan linen, and a number of books ; its walls were decorated with many fine Spanish plates. A table held a litter of small things : pens, ink, seals, and in the midst of them a piece of aged, dusty chocolate. I do not know whether this also was a relic of the Archduke's

occupation, but it certainly had the effect of human-
izing the dead nobleman.

He was a remarkable man. They say that he
spoke almost every European language, and that on
his deathbed he could not distinguish one from the
other, but spoke such a strange confusion of tongues
that only a philologist could interpret his last wishes.
He had an extraordinary passion for trees, and the
mountain slopes for miles around his lonely home
owe their groves to his intercession with the wood-
cutters. His love for trees was so intense that he
would not even use firewood from his own estate,
but bought all he needed from others.

This passion for trees cost him a great deal of
money : local landowners were not slow to take
advantage of his weakness. They realized that
whenever the woods within sight of his home were
threatened with the axe, the Archduke, to save the
trees, would buy the land on which they stood ; so
that whenever a landowner wished to dispose of his
estate for a good price he circulated a rumour of his
intention to cut down his timber. Hence the
Archduke became the owner of thousands of acres
of mountain land along the rugged coast.

The Archduke had a secretary, and the relations

between these two must have been peculiar.   Perhaps they are best expressed by the curious marble group, the work of an Italian sculptor, that occupies a room on the ground floor.   It represents an angel summoning the secretary to cease from labour. This sculpture was executed at the request of the Archduke, who on his death made it possible for the secretary to follow the angel's advice by leaving to him all his wealth !

" He was a good man, the Archduke ? " I asked the woman, who had been one of his servants.

" Ah, si, si," she said, shaking her head slowly and looking at me with mournful brown eyes.   " He is the finest man in the world."

She spoke of him as though he were still living, and I believe that to her he was a living presence in the lonely house, and that she tended his rooms and preserved his beloved plates and furniture as though he were using them every day.

She took us through a pergola to a tiny circular chapel which he had built for his private devotions, and then she showed us the pathway down the cliff by which we could reach the chapel of Ramon Lull, the Saint of Majorca.   It was on the present site of the Archduke's house that Lull established in the thirteenth century the first Christian college of Oriental languages and missionaries, and a small white chapel to his memory had been built on a desolate peak of rock over the sea. You may reach it by a rough cliff pathway and by crossing a small stone bridge which spans the deep gorge between the mountain side and the lonely peak. All around you, a thousand feet below, lie the tumbled grey rocks and the sea.

The two foundation stones of this chapel have a history. One was brought from Bougie, in Africa, where the feverish soul of the saint was beaten out of him with stones; the other from San Francisco, in California, in memory of the Franciscan who founded the city. The interior of the chapel is about eight feet in diameter, and the floor is strewn with the skeletons of birds that have entered through a broken glass in the small spire and died there, unable to find their way out.

Presently we climbed along a cliff path to the road and set off towards the little town of Deya. Still the winding road continues, sometimes high above the sea, sometimes curving inland round a cup in the mountains to avoid a descent into a deep valley. And here in the valley you can wander in the sunny

silence and pick from the trees that give you shade
the golden oranges and lemons, the cherries and
green figs that splash their brilliance over the silver-
grey rock. The Spirit sat on a boulder and for
fifteen minutes ate more green figs than were good
for her, picking them off the tree that shielded her.
Vagabonds and thieves we may have been in the eyes
of the stern moralist, but not in the eyes of the
Majorcans : these fruits are so plentiful that the
poorest husbandman will give you as much as you
can carry and expect no payment. Oranges and
lemons strew the ground in these groves like wind-
falls in a Kent apple orchard.

Through the groves we reached Deya, a town so
small that it would pass for no more than a village
in England. It lies on the side of a hill by the sea,
mounting up and up to a pinnacle whereon stands
the *fonda*, with its terrace hanging over the rest of the
town. The mountains rise up on every side, enclos-
ing the sloping town and its hill in a warm and perfumed hollow. We climbed up to the *fonda*, where
we were greeted by a little grave woman whose face
had the same settled expression of placid contentment that we see everywhere in the island.

Could she give us food ? Yes, in fifteen minutes.

She took us on to the terrace, and while we sat under a pergola of twisting vines she leaned over and called to her husband, who was working in the steep garden.

" Julio, Julio—touristas."

Julio called back to her, and presently he came up laden with vegetables : fresh lettuce, artichokes, potatoes and a cabbage. He, too, has that benign placidity and those soft, friendly brown eyes. He is lean and brown, and his hair is grey. Presently he is waiting on us in the small white dining-room of the *fonda*, and his wife passes dish after dish to him through the kitchen door.

One does not expect a banquet at a mountain village inn, but it was a banquet that these two gave us. First came wine and a vegetable soup, then a variety of strongly-seasoned sausage meats with fried cabbage. Followed the inevitable lamb chops, succeeded by a dish of vegetables. Then, chicken and a salad, a dish of artichokes well steeped in oil, a basket of fruit, and a bill—four pesetas each : half a crown each for a banquet ! Where but in Majorca would the casual caller at a wayside inn get such a meal at fifteen minutes' notice ?

There is nothing to see in Deya, and nothing to do except to be peaceful and dream away the sunny

153

days in the mountains and the lemon groves. The people work on the land, or are engaged in their grey stone houses in the normal pursuits of shoe-making, chair-stringing, and hand-weaving. We were anxious to get to Soller that night, so we started off again in the afternoon.

We had reached a point less than a mile out of Deya when there was a noise of motor-cars behind us. Round a corner of the mountain road, in a cloud of golden dust, swung a large car, travelling at forty miles an hour. It was full of men and women : the men goggled, huddled together, holding on their hats, and shouting into each others ears to make themselves heard; the women veiled, with the streaming ends of their veils flying behind them, their faces screwed up and distorted in the rush of air. The car roared past; another swung round the corner, and another. The onslaught was so sudden on the narrow road that we scuttled across into the safety of the rocks like a pair of startled hens.

And then the procession began. Thirty open cars, full of people whom we could dimly see through the tornado of dust, roared along the mountain road. Dust obscured the distant sea, obscured the sun, obscured the peaks above from the sight of God and man, and particularly from the sight of the motorists. The valleys threw back the echoing roar of their engines and the hoot of their horns. Sheep on the uplands ceased from browsing, raised startled faces, and bolted. Grey lizards flashed up the rocks, shedding their skins as they went, to hide in crevices and holes. . . . You have guessed correctly : the cars carried rich American tourists. They were " doing " Majorca.

We heard afterwards that they had arrived at Palma in the morning on a boat in which they were touring Europe. Palma had been ransacked for cars, and in these the whole shipload of Americans had set out to " do " half the island and return to Palma before sunset to board their liner, which would then take them to Marseilles.

Here they were, roaring and hooting their way through mountains which they could not see, above a glorious sea which was hidden from them, through a tract of country, the most sublime in Europe, which they could not enjoy ; and every mind had apparently but a single thought : to keep its hat on.

I think I ought to moralize here. Something in this manner : Behold, then, the peril of riches, how they hideth from man the beauties of the earth ;

how they taketh him even as the tempest and sweepeth him with great noise unto the uttermost corners of the earth, yet learneth him nothing; how they giveth him of all the fruits of the earth, yet denieth him the enjoyment thereof. . . .

★   ★   ★   ★   ★

Towards evening, when the sun was sinking behind the mountains, the road took us inland, and presently, rounding the side of a hill, we came in sight of Soller, shining white, far down in a great hollow in the mountains. Vast masses of grey rock towered up all round the town, which had the appearance of a flock of sheep browsing in a dell in the golden light of the setting sun. A dusty, sun-baked town it looked, so deep-set amid its guardian mountains that it seemed as if no wind could ever reach it. While we were standing there gazing at it down the slopes we heard again the noise of many cars.

" They're coming back," cried the Spirit, scuttling down into the rocks.

Again they came roaring past, and the faces of the occupants were still distorted into strange shapes. They were still giving all their energies to the task of keeping on their hats and veils.

We counted only twenty-nine cars this time, and it was not until half an hour later that we came upon the thirtieth. It was drawn up at the side of the road, and beneath it the driver, his face brown with mud composed of perspiration and dust, was working feverishly at the engine. Inside sat two women, very anxious women they were, and a furious man stamped up and down in the dust, saying :

" It looks like we gonna be stranded on the chunk o' rock. It looks like we gonna lose that boat, I tell you. We'll hafta chase half over Europe to catch her again. Aw, hell ! "

Whether the boat waited for them when they were missed we never heard. It is probable that, when the thirtieth car did not arrive, another car was sent back to look for them.

As we wound down into Soller the heat became more intense, for Soller is one of the hottest places in the island because of its shield of mountains. For the same reason it grows more oranges and more mosquitoes than any other town in the island. We dragged ourselves wearily through white-hot streets, where most of the doors were closed and the windows shuttered to keep out the heat ; and presently, in the shade of a little square, we found the *fonda* we wanted.

The proprietor was lying back weakly in a basket chair in the cool interior, fanning himself with a plate. He seemed utterly exhausted, and I took the liberty of presuming that the heat was too much for him.

" The heat, señor ?   No, it is not the heat, it is the   Americanos !   Oh,   los   Americanos !   They come like a swarm of flies to be fed, down on me they come—whoof !—and I have to search all the town for food enough to feed them."

We asked for rooms, and he called his manageress. He called her, as we soon discovered, not because he was too lazy to attend to us himself, but because she was his master.   She dominated everything. She was a pale, slim woman with dark, fierce eyes that held always in repose a kind of smouldering discontent.   Her voice was harsh and loud, and although she was polite enough and gave us a chilling, artificial smile, she openly surveyed our clothes with hard, calculating eyes.   We could see her mentally adding subtle items to our bill and totalling it up even before we had thoroughly arrived.   I knew our stay would cost us more because the Spirit was wearing a silk and wool coat bought in Paris.

It was the first time we had encountered this atmosphere in Majorca.   The reason was that she had received her worldly education on the Continent.   She breathed that atmosphere of suave, sinister politeness which conceals the grasping soul of the inveterate and determined money-getter.   She had the manner of a Wardour street *modiste*, and one almost expected her to say, as she took us upstairs : " This room would be eminently suitable for modom.   So very becoming ;   and the colour of the walls suits modom's complexion so well."

Such encounters as these make us appreciate the simplicity of the island character.   The Majorcan is not yet contaminated by the Midas spirit.   He likes things to turn to gold, naturally ;   but he also likes things to turn to friendship and happiness. He asks a fair price for all he offers, and you have no cause to bargain with him.   He will not cheat you because he thinks you are ignorant.   But the soul of Madame is steeped in calculation ;   she has learned all the ways of the Continental shopkeeper who caters for casual customers ;   she will take your money and send you away penniless, still with that chilling, soulless smile on her face.

But she is efficient.   She runs the *fonda*, and its proprietor and her servants in perfect harmony

The proprietor sits around and yawns between the intervals of cooking the meals, which are good, because he also has been abroad. And when we go to bed two voluminous mosquito nets of rose, made by madame, cover our beds, so that we can lie there and imagine we are sleeping under the sky.

Now Soller is notable for its mosquitoes. And I think the mosquitoes are notable for their skill in defying the nets. There did not appear to be any concealed under the nets when we entered them, but within half-an-hour the interiors of the rose canopies were humming with the sound of many wings ; a vicious, high-pitched humming. The Spirit was flapping about in the confined space and shoo-ing vigorously, but shoo-ing is not the correct method of attack upon mosquitoes, for presently she complained that her left eye was closing. The sting of a Sollerian mosquito will close anything, from an eye to a long and useful life.

Presently we conceived the idea of getting out of bed for a time and leaving the nets open to entice the blood-crazy creatures to follow us. The trick seemed to succeed, for after we had stood on the cold stone floor at the far end of the room for five minutes the mosquitoes came humming round our

ears and our ankles.   Whereupon we scuttled fur-
tively back to bed, pulled the nets around us, tucked
the ends under the mattress, and sat listening to the
thwarted insects wailing outside like disconsolate
demons shut out of their rightful sphere.

One of the peculiarities of mosquitoes is that they
seem to acquire the characteristics of the people on
whose blood they feed.   The easiest mosquito to
deal with is the German.   He is slow-bodied ; slow
in jumping-off, slow on the wing ; you can catch
him a slap of death without much difficulty.   The
English variety has similar characteristics.   But the
Latin—he is the terror of European mosquitoes.   I
think the French is the worst, for he darts in, takes
his spot of blood, and—whe-e-e—he is off and away
before your devastating hand is half raised for the
death-blow.   The Spanish is slower than the French,
but he has more persistence, a greater staying power ;
if he cannot get you at night, he will sit on the doorstep, as it were, and get you in the morning before
he goes ceilingwards to his rest.   And like the
Spanish people, he is intensely musical ; his song
has in it trills and variations which might charm
one's last waking minutes, if they did not hold so
sinister a warning.

VI.—DON JUAN AND ROJA
THE MULE

A CLATTER on the flat roof awakened us in the morning from a mosquito-haunted sleep, for in spite of our precautions there were several incursions into the nets during the night, and our faces had suffered in consequence. The clatter continued; presently something bumped up the wall of the *fonda*, and a dark object shadowed our window.

We scrambled out of bed to investigate, and found Juanita, the serving-girl, on the roof, hauling up a basket of washing to hang in the sun. She was eating fruit, and, seeing us peering up at her, she tossed two oranges into the big basket when it was empty, lowering it to our window with a " Buenas, Señora, buenas, Señor."

After she had brought us coffee we went out into the town. The heat was intense, even in early May. The streets were busy with preparations for the annual festival which, lasting for a week, celebrates the triumph of the people of Soller over the pirates of Barbary in 1561. . . . Over the mountains at night came these blood-thirsty men, stealthily over the mountains and into the sleeping town, as they had come to nearly every town in the island. They attacked in two forces from different directions, yet they failed. A local inhabitant, Angelats, came to the fore in the emergency, gathered a small army of men, and sent the pirates flying back to their ships, a howling mob, depleted by five hundred men who had sought booty and found only death. Nearly every Majorcan town has its epic of sudden midnight battles and victories over pirates, and Soller is so proud of its victory that it celebrates the triumph of Angelats every spring, with song and dance, flags and feastings. . . .

One need not explore far to realize that Soller is the garden of Majorca. Everywhere fruit grows in profusion, and the winter climate is perhaps the most perfect in the island. The town, lying in its fertile hollow in the mountains, is sheltered from cold winds, and frost is a phenomenon.

One of the most popular pastimes in the evenings is a stroll along the railway line, where we found scores of people wandering up and down the single track. This habit is not so unaccountable as it would appear to be, for the railway line is not as other railway lines. Only a few trains pass along it each day, and it is bordered by orange and lemon groves, with here and there a tall date-palm spreading its leaves in the sun; and behind the orange trees on one side of the line a mountain river swirls and bubbles among the rocks. Beyond the river, which cuts its way through a small gorge, many white houses line the banks; here you see more oranges and lemons and dates, and in February the almond spreads its pink blossom in the sun.

Then there is the gas-works. An appallingly unromantic place, you will say; but not in Soller. Where else will you find a gasometer made beautiful with crimson and white rambler roses, twining up the iron supports from flower beds beneath? We stood admiring this extraordinary transformation of a crude and ugly monster into a thing of beauty, and a young workman presently emerged from a shed, picked a few roses and presented them to us. We told him it was unusual to see rose-culture in a gas-works, but he did not appear to find anything unusual in the procedure.

I should like to lead the boards of directors of some of our English gas companies to this spot and show them what can be done with a gasometer; yet I fear they would have little sympathy with such uncommercial nonsense. I cannot imagine them looking with favour on the application of a foreman to grow roses on the gasometer or sweet peas around the coke-dumps. . . .

Away along the flat dusty road, two miles out of the town, the Puerto de Soller edges a little blue bay of the Mediterranean. Like all the Majorcan towns near the coast, Soller has its port a few miles away. In the past it was not wise to build your coast town on the coast; the raids of the Moors were too frequent, and warning of their arrival was too short. So the towns grew up a few miles inland, and to reach their prize the invaders had to scramble across the mountains in the dark, while the towns-people, warned by their outposts, planned to receive the visitors with all the ceremony due to uninvited guests.

*　　*　　*　　*　　*

We had not many days in Soller before we began to feel the oppression of the surrounding mountains. They were so near us, hemmed us in so completely, that we felt the desire to pass over them to see what lay beyond. There must be something wonderful hidden there : cold green lakes in the rocks, rushing torrents, wolves, dark and secret caverns. And so one evening we ask Madame where we can obtain a mule to take us across the mountains.

" Ah, but I can find you a mule," she cried.
" Yes, the finest mule in Soller, and the finest muleteer. One who speaks three languages : Spanish,
Majorcan, and French. Think of it ; three languages and a mule for so little money ! "

" How much money ? "

It was on the tip of her tongue to give us the
figure, but she checked herself and said :

" Ah, that I cannot say, you must arrange with
him ; but it is very little, oh, so very little. I will
send for him and you can arrange."

We had doubts about this muleteer and his mule.
We felt that he would surely be one of Madame's
minions, and who could be happy travelling with
such a companion ? We would have preferred to
go alone over the mountains, but we were warned by
several people of the folly of such a course. We
could not hire a mule without also hiring a muleteer ;
the only alternative was to buy an animal.

We were eating that evening in the hall of the *fonda*
when a little, lithe, mahogany-coloured man with a
silent, springing walk entered. He wore only a blue
shirt, dark trousers, and red *spadanias*. He had quick
brown eyes that glanced alertly from right to left as he
passed, and presently Madame brought him to us.

" Señor Don Juan Trias, the muleteer," she said dramatically, and then stood back and folded her arms.

From the first we could not resist Don Juan. He was a vivacious and sprightly elf of a man. An imp of merriment lurked in his brown eyes, and when he was serious he had the courtly manner of a fairy-tale prince. He had what the Spirit calls " laugh-lines " under his eyes, and his mouth turned up at the corners as though he were perpetually restraining a smile.

Don Juan bowed with his hand to his heart, waiting for us to speak. We told him we desired a mule to take us across the mountains to Lluch and Pollensa. We wanted a mule that would not kick or bite or be obstinate or prance terrifyingly on the edge of precipices. Had he such a mule ?

" Señor," he said, " I have a mule, so good a mule, that she would rock a little child to sleep."

" What we require," said the Spirit, " is a good-hearted beast of burden, not a nurse."

" Señora," replied Don Juan. " This mule is so good-hearted, she would allow you to share her supper-oats if you were hungry. She will climb until she falls exhausted in your service, and she would permit you to use her body as a pillow while she died."

" She sounds a paragon among mules," I said. " How much will she cost ? "

" With her master, twenty-five pesetas a day."

" It is a lot of money."

" But a good mule, señor, to say nothing of her master."

We argued the matter for a while. Twenty-five pesetas was a good price, especially as we were to provide board and lodging for Don Juan while he was in our service. Eventually we came to the following agreement : twenty pesetas a day for man and mule, the mule " finding her own food," we providing for Don Juan.

" But," said the Spirit suddenly, with a glance of mock severity at Don Juan. " I want a beige mule It must be a beige mule. I couldn't ride on any mule but a beige mule."

Don Juan was nonplussed for a moment. He looked puzzled.

" To match my coat," added the Spirit, indicating the garment she was wearing.

Don Juan hesitated, then his brow cleared.

" Ah, yes, it shall be a mule of that colour, truly,"

he said seriously. " A beige mule to match your
coat, a mule who finds her own food, with a master
who speaks French, for twenty pesetas a day—truly
you have done well, señora."

His eyes danced so that we had to laugh, and Don
Juan laughed back at us. He agreed to attend on us
at nine o'clock the following morning, and then
with another bow and a flash of his white teeth he
was gone.

When we came down the next morning soon after
eight o'clock he was already there, superintending
the food supplies that we were to take with us.
There were several large packages for us, with two
bottles of wine, and a package for himself.

" See, señora, I have found, as I promised, the
beige mule," he said, taking us to the door. " And
I have given her brown shoes to match the señora's
shoes."

The gallant fellow had browned over the hoofs
of the little mule and polished them ! The mule
was as beige as a mule could be, and she looked at
us with critical interest as we approached to inspect
the panniers that hung on either side of her. Her
saddle was a pile of black and white sheepskins.
Don Juan introduced her to us as he stowed away

the food and a large number of lemons in one pannier, and in the other our small luggage and our coats. Her name, he said, was Roja—pronounced Roha—and she was the best mule in all Majorca. Certainly she was sleek and lithe, and she pawed the ground with her little hoofs in her eagerness to start.

When all our possessions were packed into Roja's panniers we went in to settle the bill; and, as we had anticipated, there were arguments. These I need not record; they were as dull as most arguments over bills, and as unsatisfactory. In one point, however, we had a victory: Madame had put down wine as an extra, contrary to the custom of the country, and when we began to protest she forestalled her own defeat by most obligingly deducting the charge for the wine. It was characteristic of her that, having received our money, she did not bother to join the two servants who came to the door to give us a send-off.

There are three ways of mounting a pannier mule which is stirrupless. If you are very agile you may spring on from the back, like a boy playing leapfrog; or you may leap from the side, like a trick cyclist mounting his saddle; or you may more sedately climb on to a stone or a chair and from there scramble on as best you can. The Spirit chose the third method, and after much writhing and twisting found herself high on the soft sheepskins over Roja's shoulders, with her feet dangling round Roja's sleek beige neck.

Don Juan and I walked on either side, and presently we left the town and began to ascend the lower slopes of the mountains.

First the dusty road passes through the terraced olive groves, but higher up the sides of Puig Major, the loftiest mountain of the island, the road degenerates into a rough and rocky mule path, the ancient way over the mountains. And here we leave the olives behind and come to the grey rocky precipices and the icy torrents. Here we pass along the face of a gorge whose sides are rainbow-hued, red and blue and green and purple and rose ; and far below the green foamy water pours hoarsely along its rocky course to the sea.

Don Juan's eyes had been searching the sky, and suddenly he pointed to a speck high above us in the air. It seemed to be stationary, as though it were a permanent spot on a blue sky.

" He waits," said Don Juan, " for us to fall down a precipice. He is my old friend ! "

THE PORT OF SOLLER

It was a vulture, hovering there a mile or more above us in anticipation that some accident would provide him with a meal of human flesh. Don Juan knew the creature well; it always accompanied him when he crossed the mountains, he said, and never gave up hope that some day a false step would throw him at its mercy.

The presence of a watching vulture has a curiously steadying effect on the mountaineer. He chooses his steps with greater deliberation. He becomes more acutely aware of the depth of the gorge along whose side he is passing! He seeks to avoid anything that might cause a slip and so bring the ravenous beak swooping down to earth. Whenever Roja neared a perilous ledge, I observed the Spirit's eyes turning heavenward, as though she expected the vulture to begin its descent in anticipation!

Don Juan reassured her. She need not fear, he said; was not Roja in charge of her? Roja would not throw her to the vultures. Roja was too sure of herself.

And truly Roja was magnificent. She climbed steadily up staircases in the rock; she ambled round agonizing corners and along perilous ledges, where one of her panniers scraped the steep mountain-side

and the other hung over a precipice three hundred feet deep.   Once or twice she would tread on a piece of loose rock and her foot would slip an inch or two. Then she would murmur complainingly to herself, a little grumble of sound far down her throat.

" She is proud," said Don Juan, " Ah, she is proud, señora, and loves not to make a false step, because she knows she is the finest mule in Majorca. Have I not always told her so ? "

176

It grows cold now, and we are glad of the coats that Don Juan brings out of the panniers. A cloud drifts down from the peak and muffles us in a white shroud, but still Roja goes on unheeding, while Don Juan cries encouragingly from the rear—"Arr-ee-e-e-e"—in a high, strong voice. One gorge along which we pass is filled with the cloud; it looks like a great hollow stuffed with cotton wool.

Soon we emerge from the white shroud into a green plateau among the peaks. There is no wind here, no chill, and the sun is hot again, even though we are four thousand feet above the sea. Many small streams wind across this plateau, but at most of them Don Juan forbids us to drink, because the water is contaminated with the earth's chemicals. Don Juan knows all the bad streams and the effect of their waters upon those who drink. He has learned from experience. Beside one of the good streams we sat among the rocks at noon and ate, while Roja settled herself to a bag of oats. Then we went on again.

Sometimes Don Juan would disappear, and after half an hour we would see him bounding towards us among the rocks half a mile away, from some haunt where he had a friend who was a wood-cutter or a shepherd or a lone farmer. We dawdled and went astray many times, so that at twilight we were some miles from the monastery of Lluch, where we intended to sleep that night. Then rain began to fall and lightning tore across the sky.

" This," said the Spirit, " is what one might call a pretty kettle of fish—whatever that may be."

" There is shelter here," cried Don Juan. " See, the huts of the *carboneros*."

He cried to Roja and started off at a run along the ragged track. Roja scampered behind him, the Spirit bouncing vigorously on her sheepskin, and I scrambled behind Roja. By this time the storm was sweeping across the mountains. Arrows of lightning flared across the black sky and lost themselves among the peaks, throwing vast flickering shadows about us. In the dusk the grey crags flashed out dazzling white in the glare, like the pinnacles of a white city. Thunder rumbled nearer and nearer, louder and louder, until it seemed that the mountains were rolling in on us like monstrous skittle-balls to bowl us over. The mountains had become a nightmare of terrifying sound and unearthly light.

Roja was uttering loud grunts of annoyance as she scrambled over the rocks in response to Don Juan's cries of encouragement. Soon there came to us

178

the scent of burning wood, and a minute later we stumbled into the dim radiance of a fire that revealed three small round huts, built of loose stones and roofed with straw cones.

They might have been the dwellings of some primitive men who had survived up here in the mountains. As we approached, several gaunt, tall figures emerged from the doorless dwellings into the firelight and stood awaiting us. They were the charcoal-burners of the mountains, who live in the desolate places, cut off from their kind, felling trees and turning them into charcoal for the use of housewives in the towns and villages below.

A wolf of a man, more than six feet in height, came forward and invited us into one of the huts. He had a pleasant, benevolent face, and he was perhaps nearing his fiftieth year. He was dressed in rags. He followed us into the hut, and provided us with two stones for seats.

At the back of the hut, which was so low that one could scarcely stand upright, was a kind of raised altar built of rough-piled stones with straw spread upon them, blankets on the straw, and in the blankets a woman with a newly-born baby. A hard, rough couch for motherhood!

179

Large pieces of dried pig-fat dangled from the roof. Beside the bed lay a bulky sack from which dried beans spilled over the earth floor.

In the yellow light of a tallow candle the mother took stock of us and smiled. We inquired after the baby. How old was it? A week. Was it born there, on the stone couch? Yes, it was born there. It was the seventh child. Several of its young brothers and sisters had now entered the hut to examine us. We gave them some oranges, and then we talked to the charcoal-burner.

What a life it is, this lonely mountain existence! First the charcoal-burner must find a suitable place for his work, where there is an abundance of trees. Then he must build his home, making the walls of piled-up stones and the roof of straw: straw so skilfully laid that not a spot of rain can penetrate. Then with his sons he begins to cut down the trees, reducing their trunks and their larger branches to a suitable size. When the wood is prepared he stacks it in a great mound, puts fire to it, and covers the mound with earth.

For a week or more the wood smoulders, and the smoke trails slowly out of a thousand crevices in the earth, so that the mound looks like a hill with a heart of fire. Day and night some member of the family must tend the buried fire; must walk round the mound, wielding a long rake and covering with earth any crevice from which a flame may flicker out; for the wood must not be permitted to burn.

The charcoal-burner and his family live in the acrid smoke, breathe it, sleep in it, eat food that is tainted with it. Then, when the smouldering fire is burned out, they open up the mound, cool the wood that has become charcoal, and carry it by mule or cart to the nearest town or village for sale.

It is a great event for the family, this journey down into the town. Off come the ragged smoke-scented clothes. Faces and hands are scrubbed in the stream over there among the rocks; clean clothes appear from the secret places of the stone huts, and a mirror is hung on the outer wall so that all the family may make the best of themselves!

Comes a time when the allowance of trees in the district is exhausted. Then the burners become nomads, deserting their crude huts, moving on to new ground, building themselves new dwellings, and settling again for a few months. Often you will come unexpectedly upon a group of their abandoned huts, and if you you are weary or the day is far gone you may care to pass the night in one of them.

The lean wolf told us that he had spent all his life from boyhood making charcoal in the lonely places. He learned the craft from his father. It was, he said, a hard trade, but it had consolations. There was the peace, there was the pleasure of going down to the towns, there was the liberty. But there was not much money ! Twenty to thirty pesetas a week, that was all he could make from charcoal. A poor wage, he said, but a free life. He was content.

We were interrupted by the appearance of Don Juan, who shook his head disconsolately and said that the rain had not stopped, that it would be difficult to continue the journey, that he was filled with a thousand regrets and fears, and would we consider the wisdom of staying here for the night if the charcoal-burner would accommodate us ?

We had not anticipated sleeping in the mountains, for we had been eager to reach the monastery, where we had expected to sleep. But Don Juan was insistent on the danger of proceeding in the darkness and the rain.

The charcoal-burner rose like a distinguished host and in his slow, soft voice offered to place one

182

of his huts at our disposal for the night; and his wife, lying on her stone altar, seconded him, begging us not to continue the journey on such a night. There was no other course but for us to stay; we accepted the invitation.

The hut that was allotted to us was similar to the one in which we had been sheltering. We were provided with two excellent pillows, covered with a strong red and white check material, and with these and three blankets we made our beds. After we had finished the food from the panniers we said goodnight to Roja, who was tethered to a tree and covered with a piece of tarpaulin, and, removing our shoes, we went to bed.

It was an eventful night. The thunder was fading in the distance, the rain had almost ceased, but lightning still flickered through the mountains, shedding a dim yellow light through the straw roof into the hut. We endeavoured to make ourselves comfortable, and at first believed we had succeeded. Vain hope!

The pile of straw on the stones was soft enough for five minutes; but when it had been well pressed down by our bodies it became hard as the stones beneath.

Then, we had visitors. Presently the wide-awake voice of the Spirit asked, in a tone of rising indignation :

" Are you tickling the sole of my foot ? "

I denied the charge. A man, if he is sane, does not tickle the sole of his wife's foot on a stone bed in the mountains during a storm.

" Then there's something else in the bed," she said, panic-stricken.

I struck a match. At her feet I found a long grey lizard struggling to get through the pressed straw. I have never seen anybody bound out of bed as quickly as the Spirit bounded out of bed then. I released the lizard, which flashed down the stone side of the bed and into a crevice.

By the light of another match I saw six pairs of diamond-bright eyes gleaming from other crevices between the stones ; here and there a long tail flicked as its owner darted further into the secret places of the couch.

In normal circumstances the presence of lizards in one's bed might be calculated to banish sleep. Lizards are disconcerting bed-fellows. They wriggle and rustle irritatingly under the straw. They have a disturbing habit of darting from some hole, staring at you brightly for a second, and whisking out of sight again. In spite of these movements around us, however, we were soon asleep; we were weary after the day's climbing.

Several times during the night we were awakened, once by the movement of Roja, again by the vigorous raking of the charcoal-burner, then by stifling smoke that drifted through the doorway, and finally, soon after dawn, by the movements of the family preparing for the day's work. They were sustaining themselves on coarse, sour brownish bread, and coffee with goats' milk, some of which they offered to us. We ate and drank greedily, for we were hungry. The lean wolf was preparing the midday meal, throwing large pieces of fat into a stewpot and adding quantities of dried beans.

In half an hour Roja was saddled and we were ready to start. When I asked Don Juan how much I should pay for our lodging, he shook his head.

" They will not take money for the lodging," he said, " but if you will offer two pesetas for the bread and coffee perhaps they will accept."

I offered the two pesetas, and the charcoal-burner, accepting them negligently, dropped them into his pocket without glancing at them. The

185

whole family stood for a while shading their eyes from the sun as we started off, then they turned to their labours as though they had forgotten us.

Strange, lonely people they are, shut off from mankind. They seem to have little interest in the world outside the circle of their stone huts. Don Juan says they are good people; good friends, honest men in spite of their rags and their poverty, and I can well believe him.

Don Juan was blithe and talkative that morning. He made a great show of blowing his nose in order to draw our attention to an embroidered handkerchief on which his little daughter had worked his initials. The Majorcans embroider and initial every piece of linen they possess; they have a great enthusiasm for monograms. When Don Juan had duly impressed us, he bounded across the rocks and cut me a staff from a tree to assist my progress over the rocky ground.

Presently he pointed to a red cliff far below.

" Gorch Blau," he said. " The most beautiful in the mountains. Let us go."

After an hour's travelling we began to descend into a great crevice, cut through a mountain, which closed in gradually until it was no more than fourteen feet wide. Up and up rose the walls of the gorge, painted red and blue and grey; up and up until it seemed as though the strip of azure sky above were its roof. We passed along one side of the gorge on a narrow ledge of rock. Below, not more than six feet from the ledge, lay one of the coldest, greenest, most translucent pools that ever lured man to plunge and rejuvenate his tired body; emerald depths of icy purity, blue-shadowed at the sides, yet holding elusively somewhere in their greenness the rose-warmth of the towering walls of the gorge.

The gorge widens out again from this point, and presently we emerged on the side of the mountain and continued the descent until at last we reached a rough dusty road that curved through woodlands of dark Spanish oak. We had not gone far before we heard a clatter of hoofs on rock. Four donkeys appeared from beneath the trees. They stood in a row and stared as we passed, though their interest was not in us but in Roja. Roja was a young woman, and she resented the attentions of these shaggy beasts. She snorted loudly, tossed her head in contempt, flicked her tail in scorn. As soon as we had passed, a renewed " clop-clop " of hoofs told us that the donkeys were following us along the road.

187

Don Juan picked up a stone and flung it at them.

" These beasts," he said. " They have no manners and no morals. Always they worry Roja with their desires, but Roja will have none of them. She is a respectable mule, the most respectable in Majorca."

The ardent donkeys followed for half a mile, in spite of the frequent well-aimed stones that struck their bodies with heavy-sounding whacks, but at last they gave up the love-quest. Our final glimpse before we disappeared round the mountain was of four disconsolate animals spread across the road,

staring with lowered heads and pathetic, love-sick eyes at the disappearing Roja !

The way was easy now. The road wound steeply down through the mountains, and far ahead we could see sunny depths of green and grey valley sunk beneath the peaks. Soon after midday we came in sight of the Monastery of Lluch.

It lies sheltered in a fertile hollow among the grey peaks, a white refuge in the wildness of the mountains. Golden corn sways in the soft breeze around it and an exquisite peace broods over it. Roja raised her head, looked at the white walls in the distance, and quickened her pace. She knew that a cool dim stall and a feed of oats awaited her. She even started off at a trot and had to be restrained by a call from Don Juan.

The Pilgrims' Way from the mountain to the monastery is a long white avenue in the shade of trees. Down this road for centuries have come the pilgrims, seeking Divine aid at the shrine that commemorates the miraculous discovery of Lluch, or Lucas, the shepherd-boy of the mountains.

This is the legend. Seven hundred years ago Lucas was tending his flocks on an evening of summer. He was a pious youth and a dreamer, and as he wandered near a grey rocky hill he saw a light in a crevice near the summit. No ordinary light was this, such as might be made by a fire or a sheltered candle, but a soft diffused radiance.

Lucas hurried towards it, and there in the crevice

of the hill he found a statue of the Virgin and Child. Nobody knew whence it came, so that there was only one explanation for its existence—the explanation that was always given for the incomprehensible in those days of simple faith : it was a work of Divine origin, a miracle.

From that day the place was sacred ; news of the revelation was spread through the island, and the Church took possession, building a monastery and a chapel to shelter the statue, which you may still see in a curtained alcove above the altar, a grey imitation of a thousand other such statues.

It is strange that a statue of Divine workmanship should so perfectly conform to the local art of the period, and that the heavenly sculptor should have had no more original a conception of his subject. But whatever may be said of the workmanship, or of the gross deception practiced on the simple Lucas, the miracle has this to its credit : it created a place of rest and shelter in the wildness of the mountains, where the wayfarer may find a good bed and abundant food.

VII.—MONASTIC DAYS.

THE monastery of Lluch faces one side of a wide tree-shaded square. On the right side of this square are stables for two hundred horses or more, and above the stables are apartments in which some of the poorer pilgrims are accommodated. The left side of the square is partly bounded by houses, little dolls' houses, and a few minute shops, where live the families that serve the monastery : laundresses, serving-girls who attend to the needs of pilgrims, wood-cutters and the men who tend the monastery lands.

Half a dozen young women, hatless and shawled, came singing arm-in-arm along the road as we approached the main entrance of Lluch, a great arch in the white façade, through which we have a vista of a long broad passage and a cloistered garden. When we had tethered Roja to a ring on the wall we entered the archway, passed through the garden, and entered a long wide white corridor, at the end of which Don Juan pulled a chain that set a bell jangling somewhere behind an iron gateway.

After a few minutes' delay a fat and cheerful man

appeared, shook hands with us, said he was pleased to see us, and forthwith took us along the corridor to a chamber, into which he disappeared. Then the fat round face showed itself at a kind of box-office aperture in the wall. We observed that the box-office aperture had a curious effect on him; immediately he ceased to be a host and changed himself into an official.

You may have observed that a box-office invariably has this effect upon human beings; he who is in possession conceives a sense of superiority to the suppliant on the other side.

Not that our host expressed any conscious superiority; but his manner took on a degree of authoritative severity, and his countenance became serious with the awareness of his official capacity. And although he knew why we were there, he must needs ask us our desire; for what would be the use of the box-office aperture if one did not ask questions through it?

We told him we craved the hospitality of Lluch. He replied that Lluch would be pleased to shelter us, give us beds, free charcoal and salt for as long as we desired. He could have told us all this outside the box-office, but I think he felt that the invitation sounded more authentic when it was issued from the aperture !

Thereupon he crossed the room to the largest and most mysterious chest we had ever seen. Twelve feet in length it must have been, five in width, and four in depth. It was the kind of chest that might have concealed all manner of mysterious things ; the Forty Thieves could well have hidden in it. When he raised the great creaking lid he revealed a dazzling collection of snowy sheets and pillow-cases ; one thousand heavy linen sheets in the chest, and five hundred snowy pillow-cases, and heaven knows how many towels. He passed four sheets and two pillow cases and two towels through his pigeon hole. He presented us with a big iron key, a romantic key that might have opened the oaken doors of a mediæval castle. When he had bestowed on us all that was our due he closed the chest, came out, and immediately threw off his shroud of officialdom ; he directed us to our room with the air of a fatherly butler who had been with the family for twenty years. Then he left us to look after ourselves.

We soon found that the monastery of Lluch was not so democratic as one would expect a monastery to be. It differentiates between rich and poor, especially in the matter of rooms. The rooms of the poor are on the ground floor, and they are rougher than the rooms of the rich, which occupy the upper floors. After a ten-minute search through the great cool stone corridors we found our own apartment. It consisted of two rooms. The first, which had a heavy, battered door, contained two rocking chairs on either side of the window, two sheepskin rugs, one black and one white, on the stone floor, and a small table ; the window opened on to the square, where lime trees swayed in the wind, filling the room with their scent, and a fountain splashed its liquid jewels below. The second room had two great oaken double beds, over each of which hung an electric light. There were also a small iron washstand with a tin bowl, four pegs on the wall, and a window twelve inches by eight, let deep into a tapering aperture in a wall three feet thick, so that to look from it was like gazing through the wrong end of a telescope.

The Spirit's first action was to roll on the beds. She has a passion for billowy soft beds, and she still had in mind the stone couch of the charcoal-burner.

" Heavenly," she said, with a sigh.

First we set about making our beds, for although the monastery gives you shelter, it does not also offer domestic service. The guest must make his own bed and clean his own room ; he must buy his own food in the public dining-hall, unless he cares to bring a supply and cook it himself in the kitchen provided for his use. As we had no supplies of our own, we sought the dining-hall as soon as we went downstairs.

Don Juan had put Roja to rest in the stables and was sunning himself meditatively in the square. We told him we desired to eat. He shook his head.

" It is forbidden to eat yet," he said. " First we should go to service in the chapel. I am waiting to escort you."

" But we do not wish to go to service. *You* will go, and we shall go to eat."

"But it is impossible to eat. The doors of the dining-hall are locked against all during the service."

He was determined that we should go to service. Nothing would induce him to let us escape. With the glowing eyes of a religious fanatic engaged in the task of conversion he led us, like two penitents, to the door of the chapel. It was the first indication he had given us of his secret piousness. Inside, he knelt reverently with bowed head until the end of the service.

The church is lighted by bright electric bulbs. There is no monastic dimness, but a crude brilliance that tires the eyes.   It is as though the simple people of Lluch, finding a new wonder in the acquisition of electricity, had hung electric bulbs in every conceivable place :   children with their new toys. There are still old men at Lluch who have not ceased to marvel at the miracle of electric light.

Under the bright lights most of the population of Lluch were gathered : aged brown men with clear bright eyes, peasant girls who sat on their private stools in the aisles or knelt on the tiled floor, gazing with dreamy abstraction at the candle-starred altar. In an overhead gallery at the back of the chapel a choir of boys were singing shrill, metallic-voiced responses to the priest.

Religion is a vivid reality to these island people. It is not a thing to be taken out of a cupboard on Sundays with the best hat and gown ; it is as much a part of their daily life as sleeping and eating.   You may have no religion yourself, but you cannot fail to be impressed by the beauty of their faith.

When the service ended we trooped out with the

196

peasant crowd to seek food. Don Juan padded beside us to the dining-hall, and when we reached it he said :

" I will choose you a serving girl. She is very beautiful. She has dignity, and pride, and the carriage of a queen."

If she had in truth been a queen, she could not have had a nobler palace to shelter her beauty. This dining-hall, what beauty it has ! A vast, cool chamber with many windows and a floor of rose and black marble ; cream walls, lofty pillars of porphyry supporting the arches of grey marble that span the roof, and hanging lamps shrouded in rose-tinted muslin. It is spoiled only by the tables, which are iron-legged and marble-topped creations, such as you may find in any third-rate London teashop.

Here for a few pesetas you may be served with a good meal ; but the food is no longer prepared, as in the past, by the monks. The hall has been rented to a local caterer, a benevolent little old man who with his wife keeps one of the tiny shops outside the monastery entrance. Anything you care to order will be prepared.

While we were inspecting the hall Don Juan

197

searched out the serving girl whom he had chosen to charm us, and presently he brought her to us. She provided an interesting commentary on Don Juan's conception of what a queen should be. Slim and supple she was, but walking with a defiant

swirl of skirts.   Now a queen must never be defiant. She may be cold, she may be cruel, she may be revoltingly immoral and still remain a perfectly fascinating queen; but defiance is not a queenly

198

attitude. Yet in spite of this touch of defiance, Don Juan's queen had claims to some distinction. Her face was oval and pale, with features of exquisite delicacy ; her small decisive chin was held high, her big dark eyes hidden behind long dropping lids and fringes of black lashes. About her nostrils there was a kind of tremulous dilation, as though she were on the verge of being scornful about something. But when she smiled—ah, then we understood why Don Juan loved her ; such a perfectly-shaped smile it was, that showed her small white teeth and set her eyes glowing with soft fire. It was gone in a second, and again her face became a mask of scornful reserve and her skirts full of swirling defiance.

She was one of half a dozen girls who supplied the needs of pilgrims, and she was the aristocrat of the party. The others were heavier in body and mind, peasants all of them, each having her two plaits of hair hanging over her shawl. Don Juan told us afterwards that she was not a Majorcan, but a Castilian ; that she had noble predecessors ; that he thought she must have had a queen among her ancestors—or at the least a lady of noble birth. Don Juan weaves his romance round her, while we. . . eat steak, artichokes, piles of fruit, and drink red wine.

Afterwards we set out in search of knowledge of the management of Lluch. It is a matter of interest, because at certain times of the year this calm mountain sanctuary is flooded with pilgrims. The monastery is able to accommodate about five hundred of them ; the rest have to sleep where they can find shelter. Now five hundred guests suddenly flung into a monastery require a good deal of attention. They require, among other things, a thousand sheets and five hundred pillow cases and five hundred towels ; and these things have to be washed, and ironed, and folded, and mended.

We found the laundry, a three-storied building of grey stone, at one side of the monastery. It is a simple and primitive establishment. There are none of the labour-saving devices that bring pain to the wearing of collars and create jagged holes in the finest linen. In the big cool stone chamber are several great cauldrons, wherein a hundred sheets at a time may be boiled, and these cauldrons stand over deep pits, down each of which a flight of miniature stone steps leads into the mysterious blackness of a small furnace-chamber.

As we stood examining one cauldron something moved in the gloom of the empty furnace, and an old, old woman crept out of the pit into the light and grinned at us. Her face was as the shell of a walnut, brown and dry and wrinkled, and she wore a long skirt, bell-shaped, and the wide straw hat with flopping brim which peasants wear in the fields. She had but two teeth, yellow fangs rather, and these she showed to us at every opportunity.

So grotesque a figure did she make, rising out of the dark pit, that one may be pardoned for expecting her to begin a dance round her cauldron, with a black cat on her shoulder, uttering charms and incantations in tones malignant and shrill. But she merely pulled her hat on straight and welcomed us with her two yellow teeth.

There are eight of these wizened old women at the monastery laundry, such wizened, tired old women they are, who have grown too feeble to labour in the fields under the burning sun. Five of them wash and dry while three mend the linen. The drying process is conducted on the roof floor, which has been built in the form of a great loggia. The sides are open, and the mountain winds blow through the chamber while the sun burns through the roof, so that the loggia becomes a chamber ventilated by hot breezes. When the drying has been accomplished the final rite of ironing is performed on the middle floor, between the boiling and the drying.

Cleanliness seems to be attained easily here, despite the absence of those time-saving but ruinous facilities for which the best and most civilized laundries are celebrated. They tell us that much of the linen has been in service for fifteen years, an achievement surely that any laundry might advertise with gratifying financial results.

Not far from the laundry is the kitchen of the poor ; a long, lofty room with walls of white tiles and three high windows at one side. Beneath the windows, along the whole length of the room, runs a projection, three feet in height and faced with white tiles, in which are a dozen small arched openings to receive the charcoal fires. Pots and pans are placed on the top of the projection, and the cook fans the arched opening with a rush fan to awaken the sluggish charcoal into a blaze. These charcoal fires by which the people cook entail perpetual attention and unceasing effort to keep them red-hot ; the cook tends his pots with one hand while he fans vigorously with the other. In a far corner of the kitchen there is a pile of free charcoal in a large bin. There are wooden benches round the walls, where some peasant children are writhing and clamouring for the meal that their mother is cooking.

She talks to them incessantly while she cooks and fans. Several other peasant women, all pilgrims to the monastery, are also cooking their evening meals at other charcoal fires, and one or two hungry husbands are standing around talking noisily. When the food is cooked the pilgrims slap it on to plates, which are loaned to them by the monastery together with a spoon, a knife and a fork, and they carry it through into the adjoining dining-hall, where there are rows of long heavy tables and benches.

The hungry husbands were on the point of sitting down at a table when one of them spoke to the other, glanced at us, and coming to the door of the kitchen invited us, according to custom, to join the family and share the meal. We thanked him but declined, also according to custom; though we stayed a while to talk. The man told us that he had come to Lluch to make an appeal to the Heavenly powers. He swept his arm round to indicate the four little girls who were clattering their spoons on the table.

" Always they are girls," he said. " It is necessary to have a son. Yes, a son, for there are so many women in Majorca, and besides, I have a little farm, so that it is necessary to have sons. Therefore we come to ask for a son. Why should I not have a son ? " he asked with a shade of resentment, " other men have sons, yet I am given always girls. Is it justice ? Or am I being punished for some sin ? "

He poured out some sour wine from an enormous bottle and handed a glassful to me.

" Drink, señor, to the son of this house."

I raised the glass to him and then to his wife, for it seemed to me that she, as one of the parties to the production of this son, ought to be brought into the affair. Whereupon she smiled and nodded her head vigorously, thereby intimating her eagerness to assist in the production of anything that was required of her.

The heavenly powers receive such strange requests from Lluch that their ingenuity must at times be severely strained. A little while past a pilgrim journeyed there to entreat the powers to reveal to her the hiding place of a sum of money known to have been concealed by a relative who had died. But mostly they are the sick and the maimed who come, and those who droop under the weight of grievous troubles.

During our stay at the monastery the only other pilgrims, in addition to the peasants in the kitchen, were a young man and woman, brother and sister, in deep mourning. I did not learn the object of their pilgrimage, for they preferred their own company, speaking to nobody; yet their trouble must have been heavy upon them, for they sat silent and sad in their mourning, and in the dining-hall ate mechanically and without relish. We saw the last of them in the dusk one evening, as they left the monastery, walking silently up the white road towards Escorca; two drooping figures of sorrow in the glory of the evening.

Before we went to bed that night we wandered round the monastery in the dusk, for at this time Lluch attains her greatest beauty. The moon slides up over the circling mountains, and the spiry rock formations that surround the monastery change from grey to silver, and among them Lluch rises like a white palace of sleep. If you are troubled by the cares of the world, by the pains and penalties of civilization, you may find in this mountain refuge a peace that passeth all understanding. Inside those massive walls there is no sound to disturb you, unless it be the song of a nightingale that comes to you out of the night through an open window; and the only sound that is likely to awaken you in the morning will be the singing of a peasant girl who passes under your window.

At eight o'clock the smell of a foul cigarette crept into our apartment from beneath the outer door, where an investigation revealed Don Juan sitting on the floor, embracing his knees, beside a tall water-pot full of cold water which he had brought for our ablutions.

206

VIII.—EXILES AND SMUGGLERS

We left Lluch behind us on a morning of burning sunshine and cooling breeze. Roja, after two nights in the monastery stables and two idle days, was so happy to be on the way again that she at intervals executed little joyous side-skips, and as I was walking beside her I had to take precautions to protect my toes.

We had almost finished now with the rough mountain paths, for there is a fair road from Lluch to Pollensa. Once or twice we left the road to take some short cut among the rocks round the side of a mountain, and here Roja ceased her skipping; her countenance grew serious, and the solemn expression in her big gold-brown eyes was almost humorous. She chose her way among the rocks on the precipitous path with the sureness and care of a cat; but once she slowly slipped several feet down a treacherously smooth slab of rock on a path that sloped one foot in three. She stopped cautiously at the end of the slide, grumbled in her throat, and turned such an apologetic face to her master behind that he burst into a laugh, slapped her haunches, and called her " *petite fromage* "; though she was less like a little cheese than any mule I have known. The endearment seemed to please Roja, for she continued her tortuous way with a new eagerness.

This path brought us to the road again, and from here the way to Pollensa is mainly downhill. Before us for miles we saw only green and silver valleys, winding away and away among peaks and precipices. The road passed under towering walls of rose and grey rock, through lonely olive-groves, with never a sight of a house or a human being. We descended presently into one of the valleys, and here the Spirit expressed a desire to walk. Her body, she said, was stiff from the pack-saddle. She wanted to walk for miles and miles to regain the use of her legs. Whereupon I took her place on Roja's shoulders, and after eating a few oranges that Don Juan produced from the panniers we started again.

We had no sooner done so when Roja gave a remarkable exhibition of her power of logic. Hitherto she had ambled along quietly, but now she quickened her pace to a rapid and decisive walk, so that the Spirit and Don Juan were soon out of sight. I pulled her up with difficulty to await them, and presently Don Juan came up laughing.

" Have I not said she is the wisest mule in all

Majorca ? " he said. " Always she is the same. She knows she has a heavier load, therefore she goes the more quickly, to arrive the sooner. The lighter her load, the less eager is she to arrive. Oh, she is wise, this little cheese."

At this the little cheese broke into a trot, so that I was forced to deal with her firmly ; or as firmly as it is possible to deal with a beige mule when a halter is the only control I have over her.

Now the way takes us through fields of yellow corn, past a sleepy, isolated farm, across cold, clear streams and under the shade of trees. If you would experience the most perfect method of travelling, ride upon a mule, under a Mediterranean sun, along a golden road that leads down from the mountains to the sea. It is a calm, effortless progress to the accompaniment of a high-pitched metallic rhythm of minute hoofs on rock. It is free from all the anxieties and distractions of modern modes of travel, and invokes a state of dreamy abstraction that no other method of progress can invoke. It is the ideal progress for the dreamer or the discoverer. These mules of the mountains need no driving, no encouragement, and they know every rocky path from custom. They amble steadily and untiringly

209

through gorges perfumed with thyme and honey-suckle and wild orchids, through shady groves of trees whose branches bend with the weight of lemons and oranges ; then up again among the crags, so sure-footed where man can scarcely walk that the mind of the rider ceases to be disturbed by thoughts of danger or by the necessity of superintending his progression.

We reached Pollensa in the late afternoon after a seven-hour journey, during which we encountered only half a dozen people. At the entrance to the town a few children who were playing in the sun gathered round and followed us ; and as we continued our way they were joined by other children who emerged from doorways and alleys. By the time we reached the centre of the town a score of them formed a noisy accompaniment around us, shouting shrilly, laughing with their bright brown eyes, and even lifting the sheepskins to peer into Roja's panniers in search of mysteries. But soon they grew tired of us and were gradually drawn away in twos and threes by other and more exciting attractions.

There are several good *fonda's* in Pollensa, which is one of the larger towns of the island, having nearly ten thousand inhabitants, a large number for a Majorcan town to possess. It was once a Roman town, though few relics of the ancient occupation remain. The streets are narrow and winding, the houses small and white, the people industrious and friendly. At almost every window and doorway you will see the women sitting at their work, making exquisite embroidery, or weaving, or spinning crude and sticky sheeps'-wool into yarn. Many of them sing as they work, and sometimes you may pass along a street that is filled with the sound of their rich, strong voices. Pollensa is a happy town. You can feel its happy atmosphere as soon as you enter its streets ; and the longer you stay, the more strongly this atmosphere grows upon you.

We chose a *fonda* on Don Juan's recommendation. He insisted that it was the best *fonda* in the town, and he looked bitterly disappointed when we suggested that we might try another. He became even more insistent that we should stay at this particular *fonda*.

"But why should we stay there rather than at any other?" the Spirit asked.

"Why, señora? Because," he replied naïvely and with an honest grin, "if you do not you will most assuredly deprive me of the commission I shall receive for taking you there!"

Impossible to resist such honesty. We had guessed that there was an ulterior motive for his insistence, and if he had concealed it we would, without doubt, have decided on another *fonda*. Likely enough Don Juan knew this, and had calculated that his frank confession would have the effect upon us that it did have; but for all that, his frankness was none the less attractive.

Roja knew the way. She wound through the maze of narrow, noisy streets until she arrived at a small doorway in front of a large stone water-fountain on one side of a square, and here she stopped, paused, looked meditatively about her, then impatiently pawed the stone-paved street with her hoofs, while Don Juan called out in a loud voice. There was a clatter of feet upon stairs, and from the doorway emerged a very cheerful but exceedingly wild-looking young man. His head seemed to be top-heavy with

a mass of shaggy hair of a nondescript colour; his face was long and thin and pale; and his body and limbs had the lolloping looseness of a puppy. In one hand he held a palette, from which oil paint, freshly mixed, dribbled on to the ground in vivid spots of colour. He advanced towards us, waving the dripping palette in the air in a gesture of welcome, so that we were forced to edge away to avoid the shower of colour.

Don Juan came to the rescue. He ran in between us and the wild young man and raised a hand in protest.

"No, no, not yet," he cried in French. "Madame and monsieur do not require to be painted—not yet—not until they have taken the dust from their clothes, at the very least."

The young man answered in German, a language that none of us understood, whereupon he went off into a howl of laughter and replied in the most atrocious French we had ever heard uttered by anybody but an Englishman.

"Have no fear," he said. "I do not yet wish to paint you. I wish only to welcome you. Later perhaps I shall paint you."

He seized our small luggage from one of the panniers and dashed with it up the stairs. Then he remembered that he had left us behind, and clattered down again, took us by the arms, and tried to lead us up. This forced upon him the surprising discovery that a staircase thirty inches wide will not permit three people abreast to pass up it. When eventually we ascended we found ourselves in a large tiled room with many windows and balconies, where a fat and sympathetic woman greeted us. Her first act was to dispose of the exuberant young man by the very simple process of placing a hand on his shoulder, leading him to a chair, and pushing him into it.

" Your son ? " we asked.

" No, no, the Saints forbid," she answered, laughing good humouredly. " He is a painter from Austria, and mad, so mad. I have had many painters here, but none so mad as he."

" Ah, but she does not think I am so mad that I cannot paint," said the wild young man. " Look at the walls." He waved his big hand in a comprehensive gesture. " Some day they will be worth much money, and then she will be rich. Will you not, old mother ? "

" Yes, yes, some day," replied the woman, and hurriedly changed the subject.

We observed upon the walls a number of canvasses. I will forbear criticism, but I fear that the " old mother's " chances of gaining riches from them are as bright as the chances of a man who digs for gold in Piccadilly Circus. We learned afterwards from Don Juan that the " old mother," who was the owner of the *fonda*, was accepting the wild young man's pictures in lieu of payment for board and lodging. She was only a peasant woman, but she appeared to have no illusions as to the merits of the canvasses.

" She has not the heart to send him away," said Don Juan afterwards. " One year he has been here, and he is always looking for someone whom he may paint and who, recognizing the genius of his work, will pour gold upon his head. Then, he says, they will buy many of the works that hang on these walls, and the old woman will be able to sell her *fonda* and live like a rich lady. But she—well, she does not mind. She loves the boy, and she is not poor."

And Don Juan, shaking his head sadly, went off to give Roja her lunch.

We found the *fonda* as pleasant a place as Don Juan had boasted; like all the Majorcan inns, it was clean and efficient, the food was good, and the proprietress a good-hearted, contented woman, eager to please and ready to suffer any trouble to make her guests happy. She fed us sumptuously in the little white dining-room, while the wild young man sprawled all over a table next to us and talked unceasingly of his genius. After we had finished Don Juan came from the kitchen, where he had been eating, to receive his dues and to say farewell, for our journey with Roja ended at Pollensa. It was with genuine regret that we parted, especially from Roja, whose almost human companionship was a perpetual charm during the mountain journeys.

Don Juan shook hands with me, then bent and kissed the back of the Spirit's hand with true southern courtesy. Before we parted he asked us if we would mention his name to any of our friends who might be coming to Majorca, so for the benefit of any who may desire his services, I give his address : Calle de St. Cristobel, 25, Soller. But if you need him, insist on having Roja also, for there is no mule like her in all Majorca.

After we had given Roja a parting banquet of sugar and sweet cakes we walked down to the Puerta de Pollensa. This lies several miles from the town, at the end of a long straight road that runs through cultivated fields and vineyards between two distant ridges of mountains. It is a dull and unattractive road until evening, when the sun has set and the carts come rattling back from the fields carrying the families to their homes in Pollensa. Six or eight people you will often see in one cart, drawn at a terrific pace by a swift-trotting horse. The mountains on either side change their greys and greens to blues, and from blue merge into a deep purple against the rose sky; and the carts tear past you, making for the heart of the sunset.

We had not gone far before a cart coming from Pollensa stopped beside us, and the bronzed young farmer who was its only occupant offered us a lift. That is to say, he smiled and asked in what was obviously a question, but he spoke in the patois, which we did not understand. We thanked him in French, then in Spanish, and climbed into the cart.

It is no easy matter, this riding in a Majorcan cart. The seat is a plank, suspended at each end by two cords, so that it moves continually like a swing with the motion of the cart. Then the floor presents difficulties, for it is usually made of thick cords, crossed like the cords of a fishing net. The meshes are large enough to permit your foot to pass, and you are in constant peril of slipping through to the full extent of your legs ! It is essentially a floor to

218

be trodden upon with care. Until you are accustomed to it your best plan is to sit on the swing with your feet well tucked up beneath you. There is always the consoling thought that, if the cords which support the seat should snap, a strong net is spread between you and the road to catch you.

The language difficulty prevented an easy flow of conversation; the young farmer contented himself by taking occasional shy glances at us, and after each glance he would look away quickly in the opposite direction towards the mountains. When we reached the edge of the port at the end of the long road he turned into a yard, and here we parted, thanking him in one language while he deprecated our thanks in another.

The long road opens into the centre of the bay of Pollensa. You emerge suddenly on to a semicircle of golden shore, and the wide arc of placid azure sea sweeps round to the purple mountains that guard the points of the bay. White and yellow houses, dwarf houses, the homes of dolls, with blue and green sun-shutters thrown wide, cluster round the gold and azure curve of the bay. A café here, a *fonda* there, with a white and shady terrace; multitudes of fishing nets drying on the golden shore, where the bronzed fishermen sit repairing the damaged meshes; a red sail like the rusted blade of a scythe passing slowly out to sea. That is the Puerto de Pollensa; a community of fisher folk, living life as it should be lived, unhurriedly, simply, contentedly.

Yet they have their days of excitement. They were having one when we arrived, and soon we were in the midst of it. The whole of the port was alive with a strange exuberance. There was singing, there was laughter, there was the sound of many voices raised in the telling of some thrilling tale. Everybody was telling the same tale, and everybody was rejoicing; and presently we came upon two men of whom the tale was being told.

They were the centre of a great concourse of people, of men and women and children and dogs, who were going with them to the church, there to give thanks for their deliverance from death. Only a week before, we learned from a girl who belonged to the terraced *fonda*, the same concourse had gone to the church to mourn the two men whom now they were escorting. These two had gone out on the sea to fish, and a storm had risen, and they had not come back. A piece of their boat had been washed ashore. Then the people of the port knew the worst, and all the people mourned; for death in a small Majorcan town is not the private and personal sorrow of a few, it is the sorrow of all. So they had gone to church and prayed for the souls of the dead men, and the families of the lost ones had mourned and wept and received the sympathy of all the port.

Then, while the sorrow was still fresh in the minds of the people, a fishing boat came one evening into the bay, and when it reached the shallows the two men who had been dead sprang overboard and waded to the shore. The news went through the port, and the people left their homes and made a great welcome.

The men, said the girl of the *fonda*, had been stranded for a week on a small rocky island far out in the sea. They had lived on shellfish and other sea creatures which they had gathered from the rocks, and at last they had attracted the attention of another fishing boat that had sailed out from the port. Their privations had not been intense, for they were hardy men; but to the people of the port their rescue had been a miracle, and how should one celebrate such a miracle but by dancing and song and prayer?

We had arrived at the last phase of the celebrations, but we followed the crowd to church to see the end. The men looked none the worse for their adventures ; they were vigorous, brown-faced men, lean and muscular, and they laughed and joked as they dragged along the women who hung to their arms. At the door of the church a fat, smiling and unshaven priest was awaiting them. The laughter and the clatter of talk continued until the crowd began to file in, but as each woman passed through the door the laughter in her face faded into solemnity, and in five minutes there was no sound but the droning voice of the priest.

*   *   *   *   *

Many days we spent in Pollensa and its port. The peace and beauty of the place and the charm of its people held us fast, so that we were reluctant to pass on. We found that we could rent a house on the mountain slopes at the side of the port for the Spanish equivalent of a pound a month ; and, having a house, we could live in comfort on one and sixpence a day each, for in Majorca one's needs are few and food is cheap. Fish may be had almost for the asking : you may have great lobsters and

222

ROMAN BRIDGE, POLLENSA

Facing page 222

crabs brought wriggling to your door, from the boats whose sails almost shadow your windows.

Smugglers are always busy along the rocky coast beyond the bay. This I discovered in a curious way. One day we had been refreshing ourselves in a certain café which must be nameless—for fear this book should fall into the hands of the Spanish Excise Officers !—when I found that I had exhausted my cigarettes. I asked the proprietor of the café, who was by this time a good acquaintance, the direction of the nearest tobacco booth. He replied that it was a good distance away, and after a slight hesitation added that he could supply me with a packet if I cared to have them. I thanked him, and he brought them to me. They were in an unfamiliar packet, but I did not attach any significance to this until later in the day.

Now among our acquaintances in Pollensa was a handsome young member of the Civil Guard, whose ostensible purpose in life is to preserve to the best of his ability the peace, and maintain the law, of Pollensa. In the evening we met this handsome young man, and we talked together, sitting at a table and drinking cognac at threepence a glass. Presently, having a desire to smoke, I drew out my packet and first offered it to him. He looked at it; then he looked at me; and then raised his hand deprecatingly and turned away his head.

" *No, no, hombre,*" he said. " Put them away from me. Do not let me see you with them in your hands."

In surprise I asked him why. He answered briefly : " *Contrabándo.*"

I asked him why he did not arrest me.

" I have seen no cigarettes," he said, " I have seen only a packet. I do not know what it contains."

Now this seemed to me to be a simple method of evading the unpleasant necessity of arresting an acquaintance, and I wondered if he offered similar opportunities of escape to smugglers whom he found strolling into the town with kegs of forbidden tobacco under their arms. He told me that recently there had been a good deal of smuggling. The people grumbled at the high price of cigarettes, due to the monopoly held by the Spanish Government, and many of them preferred to buy the smuggled tobacco. But there was an element of humour in their preference. The smuggled tobacco at one time was cheaper than the Government tobacco, but, as with most goods that are traded illicitly,

226

its price was soon increased to compensate the smugglers for the risks that beset them. At present this smuggled tobacco is as expensive as Government tobacco, but the people still buy it, for even law-abiding islanders like the Majorcans find that peculiar satisfaction, known to all law-abiding people, in achieving small triumphs over authority.

How was the tobacco smuggled in? we asked. One friend said that fishing boats had been known to carry it from the Spanish coast; it was brought down from Andorra, that curious kingdom in the Pyrenees. Constant observation was kept along the Majorcan coast for miles outside the port, even as far down as Miramar, where the cavernous rocks offered many a hiding-place for illegal merchandise. Once there was a fisherman who frequently brought home as part of his catch a dozen large crabs. Now this was natural enough; but a certain Civil Guardsman, whose business it was to observe these things, noticed that the crabs were always the largest possible crabs, that their number never varied, and that they seemed always to be excessively lethargic crabs, making no effort to use their numerous legs for the purpose for which legs were granted to them by a beneficent Providence.

227

When the Guardsman carried his observations further he ascertained that they were dead crabs, long, long dead ; and that their shells contained, not fresh white flesh, but good black tobacco. There is a handsome income from the sale of crabsfull of tobacco.

The punishment for smuggling is imprisonment, but I do not think many pay the penalty. Our friend said they had not caught a smuggler for nearly two years ; and to judge by the satisfaction in his tone, I do not think he particularly wanted to catch one. It must be painful even for a Civil Guardsman to mar the universal happiness of Pollensa. . . .

*　　*　　*　　*　　*

Wherever beauty and peace go hand in hand with cheap living you will find English people. We discovered about a score of them in the paradise of Pollensa, settled in little homes along the coast ; they were the kind of English people that one invariably finds in those remote paradises. There was the inevitable half-pay army man and the ageing spinsters whose limited income denies them an existence in England but gives comparative luxury abroad. Lonely, lifeless women they are, pathetic in their seclusion, fostering always a belief in their

228

superiority over the natives, and with their souls still weighed down by the traditions of a remote past life as it was lived in Kensington, Bayswater, or Bath. There was one little elderly woman, thin and dried-up, whose one delight was to talk about the flat she once owned in London ; a wonderful flat it was from all accounts, which she gave up " because of the servant problem, you know." Pathetic deception ! She would enumerate the rooms of this flat, describe the furniture and how it was arranged, and tell us how very convenient it was " for the park."

Then there was an elderly bachelor who sat on a sunny terrace all day reading a week-old *Times*. His pleasure was to talk of London's clubs ; he had a passion for club news ; it was to him as manna in the desert. We had but to inform him of some change or alteration in a famous club to set him wandering happily again among the grim, cold leather armchairs in the sombre austerity of its smoke-room. Although he lived in a sunlit, blue-and-gold corner of paradise, I think his dreams were always of leather armchairs and stagnant atmospheres, where the silence is broken only by the discreet rustle of *The Times*. The scanty information

229

we were able to offer him on these matters gave him so much pleasure that we searched our minds for more ; it was good to see the glow of enthusiasm in his eyes and to know that we had lifted him back into days that were happier, perhaps more hectic, and certainly more prosperous.

There is infinite pathos in the lives of these exiles, driven as they are by poverty and pride from their own country. Each one of them has some cherished memory that brings a melancholy happiness. It may be the memory of a home once possessed, or a club, or a circle of friends now dispersed by death and the passing of the years ; it may be no more than the remembrance of a single trivial event, perhaps of a meeting with a personage of title ; but whatever it may be, it should be respected if it brings a little consolation into a lonely life.

*   *   *   *   *

It was in Pollensa town that the Spirit took her second lesson in spinning. This time it was the spinning of crude sheep's-wool into yarn. We were passing one day along one of the sunny streets of the town when we saw inside a round arched doorway an aged wizened woman sitting on a stool and making rapid movements with her hands, in which she held a curious instrument that resembled a large bradawl, consisting of an iron spike, eight inches long, with a small hook at one end and a wooden handle at the other. We paused to watch, and she invited us in, showing us how she manipulated the instrument.

She works on the same principle as the Human Spider. First she fills her lap with a bundle of cloudy, yellow wool, still sticky with the grease of its former owner. She takes the bradawl, hitches to its hook a little wool from the cloudy bundle, and with a dexterous twist throws the bradawl away from her, as though she had no further use for it. The instruments spins through the air for a yard or more towards the ground, and in its flashing course drags out many strands of wool, twisting them together by the action of its spin, and forming a yard of fine strong yarn. Over and over again the process is repeated : the hitch, the spin, the cast-away. In half an hour the old woman has a good bundle of woollen yarn.

She has been sitting there hitching and casting away for years and years ; her fingers are long and bony from constant use. They make a curious contrast to the rest of her. The body is slow with

231

great age, bent and feeble ; but the swift hands and
fingers flash with the speed of lizards and the energy
of youth. It seems as though all the energy that
has left her body is concentrated in her ten fingers ;
as though she were a corpse with living hands.

She muttered strange, high-pitched words in the
patois and held out the bradawl and wool to the Spirit.
We understood this to be an invitation to spin,
whereupon the Spirit sat down, carefully hitched,
prepared for a spin, and then cast.

For ten days afterwards my leg showed the
bruise ! The bradawl, of course, had snapped the
strands of wool and gone off on its journey alone,
leaving its woolly tail· behind it. The second
attempt was more successful : the instrument still
snapped the wool, but it did no damage to anybody's
leg ; which showed, I considered, marked progress,
though perhaps not so much in the art of her
spinning as in the art of my evasion.

By this time a small crowd of neighbours had
gathered round the door. They watched the opera-
tions with a tense interest. They gave voluble
advice and made many suggestions, all of which were
useless, for no amount of advice can teach you this
spinner's art. Success depends on the twist and the

energy of the cast. The pulling power of the bradawl must be exact; not an ounce too much, or the instrument tears itself away from the fine wool; nor an ounce too little, or it will not draw out the wool.

A score of times the Spirit cast, and at last she succeeded. At once her triumph drew a chorus of " Ah-h-h-h's " from the audience round the door, as the bradawl flew out with its tail of wool behind it. This was her only triumph; all subsequent attempts met with failure.

When we left the house the old woman produced a rusty instrument from a box and gave it to us, with a cloud of sticky wool. I think she saw an opportunity to conduct a little trade, for she held up two fingers to indicate that the cost would be twenty centimos. I gave her instead a bright silver peseta, to cover also the fee for the lesson she had given; and this she accepted with high-pitched words of thanks.

The Spirit was now on fire with an enthusiasm to spin. Nothing would satisfy her but to hurry back to the *fonda* and spend the evening spinning. She took up her position at one side of the big tiled common-room. I carefully chose a position behind her. She began to spin. People drifted in for the evening meal, and in ten minutes we had another

233

audience. By this time there were shreds and puffs of the cloudy wool scattered about the room, relics of many unsuccessful castings. The serving-girl, who had lived at Pollensa all her life, and yet had never tried her skill as a spinner, wished now to learn the art; but her attempts only added to the number of woolly puffs and shreds that rolled about the room in the breeze. Every time she cast she uttered an " Ah ! " of disappointment. A young German stood watching with curious eyes, and presently he made the effort ; thoroughly, carefully calculating the spin and the cast, until he succeeded. Then the wild young artist entered.

" Ah, I must learn this, I must learn this art ! " he cried.

Here the proprietress intervened.

" Truly you may learn it, but," she said," not in this house. I know *you*; and glass windows cost money in Pollensa. See, young friend, there is a whole empty square outside where you may learn the art ! "

Whereupon the wild young man laughed noisily, slapped the good lady on her back and sprawled into a chair, all legs and arms and hair.

The spinning practice was brought to an end by the arrival of the evening meal. Lamb chops again, lobster, fruits, wine. Afterwards we smoked a cigarette with the young German, who told us that he was a commercial traveller in toys.

Was Majorca good ground ? we asked.

" Good ? " he said. " It is useless. One of the directors of my firm came to the island once, during a tour. He returned saying that there were no toys in the island. It should be a great market for German toys. Toys ! What is the use of toys to a race who do nothing but work, and work, and work ? They do not play. They work and sing, work and sing, laugh and work and sing. In Palma, yes, I get a few orders, but nowhere else can I induce anybody to see the importance of toys.

" I go among the people to test them, to find out what might attract them. I meet a farmer's wife and show her a little toy : some wooden chickens that peck at their food when you swing a ball on a string underneath them. And what does she do ? She shrugs, and raises her brows, and says, ' My man, he breeds them.' Himmel ! What can you do with people like that ? "

He was very annoyed by this lack of appreciation.

Yet it seemed to me a rash project, this effort to sell toys to the Majorcans. Like most people who win their living from the soil and the sea, they have little time or inclination for play. Not once in the whole of Majorca did we see the people gathered together in games. The children give up their play at an early age; I have seen girls of twelve cooking the family meals; and already you have seen how the small sons of the Human Spider work with their father, learning the spinner's art while they are little more than babies. I pointed this out to the young German, but it did not console him for the wasted journey from Madrid, and presently he went heavily to bed.

*   *   *   *   *

We have lingered a long time in Pollensa; we have explored the blue mountains that circle the peaceful town and its port; we have climbed the perilous peak to the ancient Castel del Rey, that hangs on the edge of a precipice into whose depths you cannot gaze without a shrinking-back to safety; we have bathed in the icy pools that are the children of foamy mountain torrents; now it is time to pass on. But first we must return to Palma upon a small affair of business, and then we shall take train to Artá, with its vast caverns created by nature and its megalithic camps made by ancient man.

IX.—THE SONG OF THE TRAIN

To begin with the beginning of the train, the
engine : it is a vast improvement upon Stephenson's
Rocket. It was made decades ago in the Midlands
of England, and it is capable of an average speed of
eighteen miles an hour. It is a little engine, high
funnelled, and it wears important tanks at its sides.
It puffs and steams and thrusts out its tanks, as a
fat little bantam cock ruffles out his feathers to
impress his importance upon the hens.

You cannot gaze upon a Majorcan railway engine
without feeling that it is trying to impress its passengers and the toy coaches that cluster behind it
like humble and grateful dependents. Its manner
says : Watch *me* while I make ready, for without
me you are lost. You are powerless without me.
These coaches, poor helpless creatures, are useless
without me ; they cannot turn their foolish wheels
without me. Yet I will condescend to pull them ;
I will have pity on them.

The engine that was to take us to Artá said all
this and more when we reached the little terminus
at Palma through the flowers and the palms that

fill the station square. The day was Saturday, a busy one for the railway. Hoards of peasants have come from the furthest corners of the island into Palma in the early hours; they have crowded through the town, talked themselves into a fever in the market place, inspected the shops, spent a few of their hard-earned pesetas; and now in the early afternoon many of them are going home.

It is an event; everybody is excited; there is none of that calm acceptance of a railway journey as a common experience. There is a bewildering roar of hoarse voices that drowns the fussing of the bantam engine, so that it hisses and puffs the more vigorously to emphasize the importance of its social position.

Shawled women whose faces are aglow with the thrill of travelling push their purchases into the coaches, hurry away, rush back, scramble into the wrong coaches, into first-class coaches, scramble out, search for their purchases, find them, hurry with them to another coach where they have found friends and neighbours.

The station is a tumult of adventurous humanity. Nut-vendors struggle through the crowd, selling pea-nuts, walnuts and brazils at thirty and forty

238

centimes a time. Nuts are the national sustenance for railway journeys; everybody buys them; we buy some; the vendor opens my pocket and pours them in. A wet, warm bulb is pressed into the back of my neck and a pitiful high-pitched bleat sounds in my ear; whereupon a brown giant of a man behind me apologizes, laughing, and wades past with a ewe lamb tucked under each arm.

Here is a woman with a black hen imprisoned under her shawl; its head protrudes at her breast, its beak moves in hoarse and dreary protest, and its eyes have the expression of startled indignation of a hen with whom gross liberties are being taken. Here is a man with two bundles of dried fish hanging round his shoulders. One of the bundles swings out and delivers a blow upon another man's ear, but everybody laughs, nobody cares, nobody falls into a rage.

A shrill warning from the preposterous bantam engine. A final scramble of humanity. Doors slam; and swing negligently open again as the train sways and grinds its way slowly out of the station. We have begun the great adventure: a journey of forty-five miles!

The Majorcan railway coach is built for utility, not for luxurious travelling. We are in a second-class

coach, because there is no third class.   The
coach is divided into compartments by waist-high
partitions ;   the seats are narrow planks eighteen
inches wide ;   and we cannot lean back, for the
partition is so constructed that it catches the
shoulders and forces the body to a forward incline.
First-class compartments are upholstered in bright
red, but they give little comfort.

There is but one notice on the wall of the coach.
We are not asked to refrain from any of those
objectionable and dangerous habits that are invariably the subject of exhortations by railway companies ;   we are merely asked not to blaspheme.
Travellers who blaspheme in the carriages of the
railway company (says the notice), will be fined
from five to fifty pesetas, and (adds the notice), if
they cannot pay they will spend the rest of the day
in prison !   I do not know how the fine is graduated,
though one may presume that the amount will
depend upon the nature of the blasphemy ;   doubt-
less a simple God-damn would cost you no more
than five pesetas.   There is a satisfaction in having
to pay for your swearing ;   a greater relief in knowing
that by giving vent to your feelings you are defying
the law.

The Song of the Train

The windows of the coach rattle vigorously, the wheels grind and bump, and small pieces of coal from the engine, which even now will not let us forget its existence, fly in at the windows and sting our faces ; but nobody cares, everybody is happy and talkative and friendly.

When the train has attained a velocity of fourteen miles an hour each bump of the wheels jars the whole coach. They make a peculiar rhythm, these Majorcan wheels ; a deliberate and well-defined *one-two-three-four*, as though they were square instead of round. Every railway has its own particular song of the wheels, but I have heard none so regular as the Majorcan song. If you listen to the rhythm of a French train you will observe that it is usually *one-two, one-two-three, one-two, one-two-three*, with an occasional lapse into *one-two-three—one-two-three*, then back to *one-two, one-two-three*. The rhythm of the trains of the Spanish mainland is *one, two-three-four, one, two-three-four ; one* defined by separation, then *two-three-four* at breathless speed. It has less variety than the French train's song, which will seize upon some thought in your mind, translate it into words, and repeat it to you with a relentless insistence that in time threatens your sanity.

The greater variety of the rhythm gives the wheels a greater command of words and enables it the better to seize upon your thoughts. If you are in the process of some emotional disturbance, the French rhythm will find out your secret before you have travelled a mile; it will taunt you by repeating your dominant thought until the end of your journey. You may be in an agony of mind over the illness of a friend, or over a business deal or a love affair: the wheels will set your dominant fear to their rhythm and throw it back at you in ridiculous words that you would never have chosen yourself. I know a tempestuous young man who, crossing France on an urgent and emotional mission, was tortured all through that long and weary night journey by the absurd and melodramatic words: I've-lost, her-I've lost; I've-lost, her-I've lost; from which you may easily gather the nature of his mission.

But the Majorcan train will play none of these tricks upon you. The rhythm of the wheels is so stolid, so practical and matter-of-fact, so unimaginative, that words will not fit themselves to its beat. It is incapable of seizing upon your thoughts and hammering them out for you against your will; you may travel in peace, with your thoughts undisturbed, immune from the brutal mockery of the French train.

*　　*　　*　　*　　*

There are many diversions for the traveller on a Majorcan railway journey. The first occurred soon after we left the terminus. A swarthy, unshaven fellow with a long thin cigar between his lips appeared with disconcerting suddenness on the footboard outside and thrust his head through the window.

" Buenas . . . Boletas . . . Boletas . . . Gracias, gracias, señor."

He grins amiably as he thrusts his arm through the window and snaps his ticket punch. Tickets are handed along the compartment, he glances at them, clips them, collects those whose owners alight at the next station, then swings off along the footboard, hanging perilously to the hand grips, the wind blowing through his hair and sending behind him a trail of vicious smoke from his cigar.

Nor is the footboard restricted to his use. Any passenger may open the door of his compartment and swing himself from end to end of the train, if he should desire an airing or a conversation with some friend in another coach. We looked from the

243

window when the guard had gone and saw half a
dozen men standing on the narrow footboard,
everyone with his head through a window, talking
vigorously to an acquaintance while the train bumps
its way across the island. The guard is an agile
fellow; he does not drive the footboard conversa-
tionalists back to their compartments so that he may

pass, but swings perilously round them and goes on
without interrupting their social intercourse.

And all the while the railway winds through the
valleys, avoiding the blue mountains, for tunnels are
costly and difficult structures; why should one go
through a thing expensively when one can so easily
go round it cheaply? This must surely have been

the argument of the engineers who built the railway, for you will see that they meticulously edge away from anything in the nature of a hill. They build economically, knowing that a railway in this island of peasants would not prove too profitable a venture ; and everywhere one may observe the care with which they have eliminated the unnecessary.

The level crossing is a masterpiece of economy. There are many of them along the track, each with a small white cottage to house the wrinkled old woman who is its guardian. When the train bumps its way towards the crossing you may see her emerging with a small flag in her hand. Her task requires little strength. She has no levers to manipulate, no heavy wood frame to swing out. She takes a cord that is attached to a post, walks across the roadway, and hitches it to another post ! That is her gate, and she has closed it.

When the train has passed she rolls up her cord and the crossing is clear. Sometimes the " gate " has little strips of coloured cloth or paper attached at intervals, like a bird-scare in a garden, for fear you should not see the plain undecorated cord ! And the old woman is unfailing in the practice of her important ritual ; there may be neither man, woman nor sheep within ten miles of her, but still she will stretch her piece of string across the road.

The train stops at Inca, and when the grinding of its wheels has ceased we hear the sound of high words in the next coach ; high words from a woman, and protesting, conciliatory words from a man. Then from the coach steps the man with his two bundles of dried fish.

He is one of the finest of the island types : tall and lean and strong, eyes shining with his vitality, a quick, flashing smile, features mobile, expressive, and stamped with the fineness of old Rome. He puts his head in at our window and speaks in the patois in a hoarse, rapid voice, with a laugh breaking through his words. The other travellers laugh and look at us expectantly, and one man asks me in Spanish if we object to travelling with fish.

We sniff simultaneously. No, we do not object. Why should we ? The fish is good.

" It is good, yes," he replied. " But there is a little trouble in the next coach with a woman. She comes from Alcudia, where her man was a fisherman. He was drowned, and now she will not suffer fish. She will not eat fish, nor look at fish, nor travel with fish. Ai ! it is a pity, with so much fish in Majorca, and so cheap."

Since we do not object, the fish is tossed under the seat. It is such dry fish that one imagines it would soak up a full bucket of water ; it is like very old

parchment, crumbling and dusty, and in dust it lies under the seat.

We all begin to eat nuts, and in ten minutes the floor of the carriage is half an inch deep in shells that rustle like autumn leaves with every movement of a foot. There are eight in the carriage, all men with the exception of the Spirit and the woman with the hen. She has taken the bird from beneath her shawl and is holding it in her lap, where it slowly droops off into a doze, awakening occasionally to utter a shrill and startled protest.

One of the men, a brown fellow whose face is sullen in repose but merry when he smiles, says that perhaps the hen is laying an egg. The woman replies that it couldn't start laying early enough for her ; she lifts up the hen and looks in her lap, but there was no egg. Everybody laughs.

So the journey passes, in talk and nut-eating, until the train reaches Manacor. Here the owner of the dried fish appears again, this time with a bag of gawdy sweetmeats, which he passes round the compartment, presumably to express his thanks for the guardianship we have established over his fish.

Every time we stop at a town the train loses a coach, so that for the final stage to Artá we have but two small coaches packed with chattering, laughing, gesticulating humanity. After we have passed Manacor the Spirit produces a map, and this creates a new and profound interest. We spread it on our knees, and the other travellers join us in our scrutiny with the eagerness of children concentrated on a picture book. One of them, an old man with thick black hair, has never seen a map of his island ; he is surprised at the size of it and the number of its towns and villages, for the map is on a large scale, showing every hamlet and farmhouse. He sits back presently and meditates with a little rapt smile ; I think he feels a stirring of pride that Majorca is so big and important-looking and bright-coloured.

The train emerges from a labyrinthine way through close-packed mountains, where it has been twisting and turning for a quarter of an hour ; the engine screams ; the hen clutters ; the peasants begin to gather up their goods ; our Roman friend swings himself along the footboard and claims his bundles of dried fish. Artá at last.

X.—EXPLORATIONS

THERE are two men, the owners of *fondas*, who always meet the incoming foreigner at Artá. One is tall, fat and self-assertive ; the other is thin, quiet-voiced, almost apologetic. Although the self-assertive fellow forces himself to your notice by his determination to get you, the quiet old man attracts you by his gentle manner and the expression of mild inquiry in his eyes.

The big man boomed towards us possessively, flourishing a card on which were set forth the advantages of his house.

" *Fonda, Fonda.* The best in all Artá."

The little mild man trotted towards us with the air of a dog that wishes to be taken notice of, but is not quite sure of the reception it will get.

" *Antigua Fonda, muy antigua.*

That is his master stroke, the *antigua*. It is printed on the card which he produces tentatively in the hope that we may care to confirm his boast. *Antigua!* He knows that foreigners, for reasons that are obscure to the big man, will invariably choose to stay in a house that is ancient rather than in one that is new, and this knowledge he uses to good

effect. The word *antigua* he regards as his talisman ;
it is a magic word that no foreigner can resist ; yet
it is not the only magnet that draws travellers to
his house. His manner is the greater attraction ;
there is a gentle, old-fashioned courtesy about him
that substantiates his quiet boast of *antigua*. In-
stinctively we turn our backs on the big possessive
man and accept the hospitality of the Friendly Dog,
who trots beside us while his rival loudly jeers,
thereby revealing his chagrin and the smallness of
his nature.

Later on we discovered that the little man is
nearly always the winner in these encounters. It
is a common fallacy that the qualities revealed in
the big and possessive man, usually summed up by
the vulgar but expressive word " push," are the
qualities that win success. This big innkeeper has
enough push to move Puig Major, yet he lacks the
one quality that transforms push from an ineffective
expenditure of energy into a force : he lacks
personality. One hears him and sees him, and
there is an end of him ; whereas one scarcely sees
or hears the little man, yet one feels his presence
all the while, even though his personality be only
that of a friendly dog.

The Friendly Dog, then, took our packed umbrella case and led us out of the station and through the little town that lies whitely on the side of a hill, climbing to a peak whereon a preposterously ugly church rears its clumsy tower. We had not gone far before we were surrounded by the largest crowd of child-followers we had yet attracted in the island. They examined us and romped round us; the shrill chorus of their voices grew wearisome.

Presently the Friendly Dog stopped and began to address them. He spoke in the patois, with a little reproving smile; he delivered a mild lecture on the ethics of receiving visitors; and in thirty seconds he had the crowd gaping up at him in silence. His power to quieten them was remarkable, for they were wild and impudent children. I do not know all he said to them, but when we continued our way they remained at a distance and gradually dispersed. If he had spoken harshly they would have tormented us the more, after the manner of children; but his gentle chiding conquered them completely.

The *Antigua Fonda* enjoys its age in a narrow street far up the town. Its antiquity is advertised by a glass sign displayed over the door; it is further advertised by the odour of the drains.

I suppose the house may be a few centuries old.
It is cramped in among the other low houses in the
street, and its dark entrance hall is lined with the
chairs of hospitality, like any other Majorcan home.
The narrow stairs from the entrance hall wind up
to another dim hall, on each side of which are three
small bedrooms with low ceilings, red-tiled floors,
and wooden beds that creak abominably when we
sit on them.   The whole place is very dim and cold,
in spite of the heat of the day.

Presently the Friendly Dog came up and asked
us whether we had any special preferences in the
matter of food.   We told him we could eat anything
except garlic and tomato.   He said he would tell
us what there was for dinner, which he called *cena*, or
supper, and then he trotted away and we forgot him.

But five minutes later he reappeared in the company of a plump smiling peasant woman and a shy
Madonna-like girl, each of whom held an array of
dishes on which were displayed a variety of uncooked
foods.   He asked us to make a selection.

This was a distinctly novel method of ordering
dinner—to select in your bedroom the food you
would eat later in the dining-room.   There were
the inevitable lamb chops, a good assortment of

vegetables, rice, fish, and fruits. We made a selection, and the three went away in single file down the stairs, carrying the piled dishes like high priests conveying a votive offering to the altar of their god.

It is a curious custom, and for a time we discussed it, trying to decide upon its origin. I developed an ingenious theory that it was a relic of the days when kings and nobles employed food-tasters, and poison was more freely administered than it is to-day:

255

the commoner, unable to afford a taster, would examine the food himself before it was cooked. But the Spirit declared this to be nonsense.

" When you go to an inn," she said, " you are taken to inspect your bedroom before you sleep in it, just to see if you like it. Why shouldn't the same principle be applied to food ? "

This was an explanation whose sound practicality put an end to any romantic and unconvincing theories.

When we went down in quest of the food we had chosen, we were led out of the entrance hall through one small tomb-like dining-room into a second tomb-like dining-room. It was evidently a room reserved for guests who might be regarded as distinguished, and we were compelled to express our preference for sociability. The Friendly Dog thereupon took us into the outer room, where we sat at a long table with two men, one of whom surprised us by expressing the following greeting in English :

" Very much like to see you, thanks. Yes ? Could be happy revealing for you all things of Artá, that is very not-interesting town when you know ! "

We thanked him for his good intentions and fell into conversation. He had a wealth of information

256

but little power to express it. He told us that he
was an Official of the State. He was appointed by
the Government to take Charge of the Government's
Postal Service between Palma and Artá. He was,
in short, a post-office clerk! He was a pleasant
little man, eager to be of service to us, and we
listened patiently while he told us everything we
already knew about Artá, and gave us a list of all the
things we had already planned to see.

Afterwards we went out into the town and looked
upon it from the church at the top of the hill. All
round the church there are great walls thirty feet
high, on the top of which one may walk to take the
air and view the country. Artá lies below, a white
crescent of a town half-circling one side of the hill,
with flat-roofed houses in the style of the Moors.
Here and there a tall palm rears its drooping leaves
above the houses. Rising up and away on every
side are the blue mountains, nothing but mountains,
and in the dusk the perfect crescent of the town looks
like the moon fallen to earth.

At night the narrow streets are thronged with
strolling women in their shawls, with their long
plaits of hair hanging down their backs. Up and
down, up and down they go; they have no other

257

amusement; they walk and talk and stand about in groups, and the streets are full of the sound of their voices. There is no other sound in all the town but the clamour of voices in the night air.

Artá has none of the charm of Pollensa. It is enveloped in an air of poverty, and most of the houses are mean structures, many with bare earth floors. The people are engaged mainly on the land. There is a small market that is conducted almost entirely by women, a dull market that offers for sale little except the bare necessities of life. Undoubtedly the official of the State was right : Artá is very not-interesting.

The next morning, after the Friendly Dog had taken us on the flat roof, pointed out to us everything of interest within sight, named every mountain that had any pretentions to greatness, and proudly emphasized the antiquity of the *fonda* by drawing attention to the weather-worn state of the stone parapet, we started for the great stalactite caves twelve miles away at the coast, and on the way a slight diversion brought us to one of the stone camps of the ancient and obscure Iberians.

It circles a rocky hill, and its walls of gigantic stones, plied one upon the other, are in places half concealed by the growth of trees and bushes. There has been no attempt at preservation; there is no necessity for preservation; this monument to the crude strength of ancient man, whose little life and whose unimportant battles have never been recorded, has been preserved by virtue of its own colossal strength.

We enter the encampment by a gateway ten feet high : two perpendicular pillars of stone with one massive stone thrown across their tops. The two great upright stones have not moved one inch from the perpendicular in four thousand years. There is a wilderness of broken rock inside, and away in the centre the great conical mound, the point of vantage, the heart of the fort. We climb to the top, sit down, and try to get the atmosphere of the place by repopulating it with the ancients who so long ago built this indestructible gateway and lifted these massive stones one upon the other for their protection.

The predominant thought of these primitive men was self-preservation; the walls express their thought and tell the story of their fears. Self-defence, which to them was an actuality, always present in their minds, has become to us a more remote necessity, since we pay taxes to have other people protect us. To them preservation was a

259

matter of strong walls and a heavy club ; to us it has
resolved itself into the possession of a banking
account. We have shifted the responsibility; we
club our enemies with gold coin and long credit ;
we even protect ourselves from the elements on the
instalment plan.

Yet it seems that in this matter of defence, civilization is leading us back to a primitive basis. The
day when fighting was the doubtful privilege of
mercenaries has passed ; the day when it was the
honour of a few selected men has gone ; conscrip-
tion is reducing us again to the tribe-war, wherein
every man takes up his club in defence of the
stronghold.

*   *   *   *   *

The lonely road to the caves winds first through
a cultivated plain, but becomes rough and uneven
when it leaves the fields for the barren rocky land.
We passed a family of charcoal-burners as we
approached the coastal mountains : two men, several
boys, two wild, half-naked little girls, and two
women, one of whom was washing herself in the
sunshine outside the stone hut.

Presently she seized one of the boys and began to
wash him also. He protested, in the manner of

260

little boys, with loud yowls and whimperings ; and the girls immediately took fright and scampered away defiantly among the rocks. We could see them peering out, maliciously enjoying the sight of their brother's torture ; but when they caught sight of us they forgot the suffering boy and began to follow us, circling round us among the rocks and keeping themselves hidden whenever we turned to look at them.

They kept this up for more than a mile, and nothing would induce them to come near us. We rattled some copper coins. This attracted them, but they would not approach near enough to take the tempting pennies. The lonely life these children lead amid the rocks and the pine-woods makes them shy of strangers ; they are as timid as fox-cubs and as wild as wolves.

We lost the children soon afterwards, and then, through a grove of pines, we came upon the most exquisite bay in all Majorca. Blue mountains enclose it, pine trees grow down to the golden sickle of sand where a turquoise sea ripples in to meet the mountain stream that sparkles across the shore. Sunshine, and silence, and loneliness ; the world of men lost and forgotten ; not even a house to

261

destroy the illusion of universal peace. It is untouched, unspoiled; for once nature has escaped the improving hand of man.

One wants to play at Robinson Crusoe here! One wants to play at desert islands! One wants to make love, to be romantic, to dream all the impossibly-coloured dreams of youth! You who have craved for an island in the South Seas need go no further than this bay; here you will find air as languorous as any that the Pacific can offer. You who loathe the sight and sound of man may escape him here—until you hear the crowing of a cock away there through the trees. You know then that man is not far from you.

We went in search of him and found woman, fat of body and shiny of face. She came out of a little white hut at the foot of the mountain that guards the left point of the bay, and when we asked her the way to the caves she called to a youth who lay sleeping under the pines at the back of the hut. He scrambled to his feet, rubbed his eyes, and informed us that he was a guide.

Now as a rule we have a strong objection to guides. They are the curse of explorers. Their mechanical claptrap is fatal to the atmosphere of romance you may be trying to capture; they insist upon telling you all the things you know and none that you wish to know. They think that unless they maintain an incessant babble they are not earning their money. Few of them understand that there are moments when silence is imperative for full enjoyment. Yet in the matter of the caves it was wiser to have a guide. Parties have gone alone into the heart of this mountain, we had heard, and have never come out of it. We therefore accepted the youth's services, but we determined to deal firmly with him if he should attempt to spoil any effects by unnecessary explanations.

He was silent enough as he led us up the narrow path that climbs round the side of the mountain. Through pine-woods it climbs, through rocks red and grey, until we are out of the bay and high above the open sea on a precipitous ledge. The path curves round and up the mountain-side for a mile, and suddenly we are face to face with a vast, dark cavern in the side of a rose-tinted precipice. The entrance must be forty feet high, and beneath it are fifty or more steep, rough-built steps by which we mount from the perilous pathway.

We climb and peer into the blackness but can see

nothing.   It is a terrifying cavern, vast, black, silent.
It might be the lair of a mythological dragon, and that
ledge below might be the spot where beautiful virgins
were tied for the annual sacrifice.   Anything might
come out of this cavern, so silent and mysterious it is.

The youth disappeared in the darkness and
emerged with an acetylene flare, from which he
succeeded in producing a light after ten minutes of
experimenting.   He held it above his head and we
followed him into the cavern.

Immediately the black silence of the mountain
closes on us.   The cavern is so enormous that the
acetylene flare becomes as insignificant as a candle.
At our feet we see the beginning of a flight of rocky
stairs, steep and without handrails ; on either side,
black depths of space.   Down we go, down into the
heart of the mountain, deeper and yet deeper.   The
great hole in the precipice through which we have
just entered has diminished to the size of a saucer ;
now it disappears entirely, the steps come to an end,
the acetylene flare sputters and goes out.

In the darkness we can hear the soft movements
of the guide as he fumbles to re-light it ; but we
hear something else—the drip of a thousand separate
drops of water.   Loud, bold, infrequent splashes ;

soft, rapid patterings, like a multitude of tiny feet running across the rock ; little hissing whispers ; then, from a distance, a loud gurgling chuckle, like the malicious laugh of a demon hiding in the darkness.

The light flares up, brighter and brighter until it dazzles. And then the beauty of the place begins to be revealed. We are in a great hall, a cathedral ; pillars rise up to the invisible dome, pillars so immense that you cannot circle them with your arms, pillars slender and fluted and knotted ; columns that sparkle like jewels, throwing off emerald and ruby lights. At our feet is a round heap of hard black basalt that flashes light from a million facets.

The guide passes through an opening at the far side of the cathedral, and we are in another cavern. We pass from cavern to gallery, gallery to corridor, corridor to cavern for more than a mile in the depths of the mountain, and everywhere we thread our way through gigantic stalactite pillars ; everywhere we hear the unending patter and whisper of the mineral rain that has been building these pillars through unrecorded ages of the past and will continue to build them through the aeons of the future. Some of the stalactites are more than a hundred feet in length, reaching from roof to floor ; and only

265

when you know that a growth of a few inches may be the work of a thousand years will you realize the millions of years that have gone to the making of some of these gigantic pillars.

Some of the columns are in the process of formation : the stalactite is growing down, the stalagmite growing up to meet it, and there is a gap of ten feet between the two. Ten, twenty thousand years may pass before the two are joined. Then the process of thickening will begin ; a hundred thousand years, and perhaps the perfect column will have been formed.

We cannot gaze upon these stupendous creations of nature without a sense of wonder. We have come to regard the architectural creations of man as the supreme art of the builder ; yet the power of man is dwarfed by the power of a single drop of water that, repeating itself through the centuries, has built these pillared halls in the heart of a mountain.

While we are here, inside the silent mountain, let me tell you the story of the part these caves have played in the deliverance of Majorca. Seven hundred years ago, when King James the Conqueror was driving the Moors out of the island, his victorious troops swept up to Artá in pursuit of the enemy. Down the valley to the bay fled the retreating Moors,

266

fifteen hundred panic-driven men with their women and children, their cattle and their wealth; behind them the avenging army, before them the sea—or the caves. They chose the caves.

Into the heart of the mountain went the men, with their women and children, their cattle and their wealth. They were safe here, for no army could reach them. They build a palisade round the mouth of the entrance, and there they spent their days in the dripping silence, waiting, hoping for heaven knows what miracle to deliver them.

James was checked, but only temporarily. One night two of his officers, concealed by the darkness, were lowered by ropes down the cliff to the wooden defences at the cavern's mouth. Carefully, silently they worked, and presently a flame leaped up, then another, until the defences went up in a blaze.

Inside the mountain, fifteen hundred men, with their women and children, their cattle and their wealth, coughed and choked in the darkness as the smoke drifted in on the breeze from the sea; smoke that swirled from one cavern to the next, slowly and filled the heart of the mountain. They fought against it, but there was no hope, nothing for them but surrender, and soon they filed out, with their cattle and their wealth, leaving the caverns to the patter and whisper of its architectural rain.

* * * * *

When we emerged from the mountain we were ravenous, for the air of the caverns is cold and invigorating. Our guide told us that his mother would prepare us a meal, and when we reached the small white hut at the bottom of the mountain slope we went into her kitchen to find out what she could give us. *Paella, pollo, fruta, vino.* Good.

We went out and sat at a rough wooden table in front of the hut and beneath the pines at the edge of the rippling bay. While we sat there talking, we heard the sound of a vigorous pursuit among the pines. A moment later a distraught fowl fluttered and squawked round the hut, pursued by the youthful guide. The chase circled our table ; then the unfortunate fowl made off towards the other side of the bay. The youth followed, grimly determined. He was catching our lunch.

It is an exciting experience, watching one's lunch being caught. When one's lunch possesses wings, there is always a doubt whether it will be caught ; and when one is hungry this uncertainty gives a greater interest in the chase.

We watched anxiously. We saw our lunch dart among the pines, then out again to the shore of the bay. It bore along the water's edge and here it gained considerably, for the soft sand increased the difficulties of pursuit.

Back again to the trees ! Here the pursuer tried cunning ; he paused, nonchalantly put his hands in his pockets, and gazed casually around him as though the thought of capturing a fowl had never entered his mind.

Our lunch cocked its head, stared at him suspiciously, and passed the time of day by giving a desultory peck or two at the ground. The pursuer looked at the lunch out of the corner of his eyes.

A quick dart ; a squawk and a flutter ; out on to the sands again ; through the stream ; round the hut ; up the first slope of the mountain and out of sight !

The old woman appeared at the hut door and cried shrilly to the youth to hurry himself. She was answered by a triumphant shout, and presently he came scrambling down the slope with the fowl in his arms. The old woman took it inside her hut. After a few seconds there was a hoarse, wailing cry, followed by an ominous silence, and we knew that the bird would be pursued no more. But the

269

incredible thing was that in fifteen minutes its flesh
was served up to us ; the bird had been plucked,
prepared, and cooked in so short a time that we could
scarcely believe it would be eatable. Yet it was
excellent, cooked to a rich brown and shining with
olive oil. We enjoyed it, even though we had
watched its heroic struggle for survival and heard
its death-cry. Hunger has no respect for hyper-
sensitive scruples.

When we were preparing to leave, a car came
bumping through the pines, and a bulky young man
with a girl alighted, demanding food. We talked
to them for a while. The man was a Castilian, the
girl a Parisian, and they were obviously lovers.
They told us they were exploring Majorca by car,
and while they talked they continually caressed each
other in an embarrassingly open manner.

We had a last glimpse of them before we were
lost in the pines : they were sitting at the table,
making love to each other while they waited for a
meal. And around them the youth was noisily
pursuing another lunch, though they did not appear
to notice the chase, so obsessed were they with their
own delightful affairs !

We travelled the last three miles back to Artá in

a cart with two young farmers and a bag of fish. We saw their string-bottomed vehicle coming up behind us at a great pace, and the Spirit was tired, for we had walked nearly twenty miles.

" I'm going to take a lesson from Watts," she said. She climbed on to a wayside stone, sat wearily upon it, and became immediately a modernized tableau of " Hope."

The cart came on, the young farmers gazed ; the cart passed, stopped, returned, and we were invited to ride.

The last string of the lute had held !

XI.—ISLAND FOLK SONGS.

WE had our first introduction to the folk songs and music of the island during a noisy journey from Artá to Inca by diligence. At the last moment before we started, an elderly man who had the litheness and vigour of youth ran up to the diligence and scrambled in, breathless and laughing. He held a sackcloth bundle in one hand, and in the other a Spanish guitar. He talked volubly for ten minutes after the start, telling anybody who cared to listen the reason for his hurry, telling where he was going, why he was going there, and when he proposed to return. The Spirit began to examine his guitar. He handed it to her.

" Play to us, señora, play," he shouted above the rattle of the diligence.

She laughed and told him she was not skilled in the use of the instrument.

" You shall play to us," she said.

" Yes, yes, play to us," came the chorus from the other passengers.

He needed no other invitation, and he began to strum the guitar. He played little sad, slow melodies, and presently he began to sing, in a deep rich voice, some of the songs of the peasants.

We were not able to gather much of the verses during the noisy, jolting journey, but afterwards, when we reached Palma, we collected some of the words and music with the assistance of Señor Don Antonio Pol, the Majorcan composer, who has made a study of the songs of the island and published a number of the melodies. We have him to thank for these reproductions.

In these songs you will find the complete expression of the character of the Majorcans in all its primitive simplicity. Many of the melodies are inspired by the music of the church, whose influence upon the people is strong. The words express the simple daily thoughts, and the occupations, the hopes and fears and troubles of the people. Few of the songs contain more than one verse, which is repeated until the singer grows tired of it.

One of the simplest and most typical is the Song of the Olives. The olive has been extensively cultivated in the island for more than a thousand years; some of the most inaccessible mountain slopes are planted with the trees; and the gathering of the fruit for centuries has inspired the following verse, which the picker drones over and over as he clings to the branches and drops the olives into the baskets:

TONADA DE S'ETSECAIADA

CANCIÓN DE LOS OLIVOS

3.

Lent

Jo es _ tio da _ munt d'un ci _ mal El mes

Es _ toy del al _ to o _ li _ v _ ra _ en pos _

alt de s'o _ li _ ve _ _ ra Feis ple _ ga _ ri _ es a _ mor

tu _ ra pe _ li _ gro _ _ sa pi de al cie lo oh mi her _

me _ va Que si caig nou fas _ si mal.

mo _ sa que si cai _ go no me _ hie _ ra

> I am in the olives high
> In a seat so perilous,
> Pray to heaven, oh, my fair one,
> That I hurt not if I fall.

Almost every occupation of the islanders possesses its own special song. The thresher of corn sings to his weary horse in a long-drawn, mournful wail, as with lagging steps the beast of burden plods round, threshing the grain from the ears. He sings mournfully because he has memories of the days when his horse was a noble animal instead of a decrepit hack; and because, perhaps, he now cannot afford to buy another horse. His song begins with a high, thin wail, and ends with a sustained " Ar-e-e-e-e-e," urging the animal on to further efforts.

> Ah, . . . – – – – – – – – – – – –
> My horse, my little horse,
> Once a fiery charger
> Ah ! . . . Arr – e – e – e – e – e
> Now you are a hack with bones,
> A hack with bones that pierce your skin
> Ah ! . . . Arr – e – e – e – e – e.

I have already spoken of the inevitability of lamb chops in the island diet, and of the primitive weaving of wool. I have not been able to discover a weaver's song, but the shearer has a special melody of his own, and the words of his song express an ingenuous

276

CANÇÓ DE'S BATRE

CANCIÓN DE TRILLA

surprise and pleasure at the discovery that he can sing and shear at the same moment, thus :

> The shearer shears his sheep so well,
> So skilfully he wields the shears,
> That while he works he sings a song—
> Now the naked flesh appears !

The song of the Love-Sick Daughter expresses the inevitable cry of all love-sick daughters in all lands—the yearning of a maid for a man who is oblivious to her passion.

> *Mother :*   What do you long for, daughter mine,
>   A dress of fine embroidery ?
> *Daughter :* Ai ! Mother mine, I seek no dress
>   Deeper far my sadness lies,
>   In the aching of my heart.
> *Mother :*   What is it, then, my daughter,
>   Do you seek a handsome youth ?
> *Daughter :* Ai ! Alas, I die for him
>   For my sadness is of love,
>   Only he can soothe my pain.

One of the best examples of the Moorish influence in the island music is the Song of the Zambomba, a curious instrument which may sometimes be seen and heard at *fiestas*. It is constructed on the same principle as a drum, but is pierced by a reed, which is rubbed vigorously with moistened hands to produce a deep, vibrating boom of sound. The insistent rhythm of the East runs through the music, exciting the listener, spurring him into wild and passionate dance.

278

OUT OF THE SUNSHINE

THREE short, piercing blasts of a siren; the cluttering of a thousand fowl; the bleating of a goat; the stamping of five hundred frightened rabbits. *Rey Jaime* is casting her moorings. We are leaving Majorca.

The boat is crowded with chattering humanity, and the sides of her decks are piled high with crates of livestock. We edge past the saloon to the upper deck, avoiding the protruding heads of the indignant fowls that are going on their first and last journey to Barcelona. Pale nervous eyes of rabbits peer at us from behind the wooden bars of their prisons. A goat lowers her head with a menace of horns, runs forward with malicious intent, and is arrested with a jolt by the chain that holds her to the taffrail.

The sound of a guitar is heard from the shore, growing fainter across the slow-increasing space between boat and quay. The musician is a tall brown fellow, surrounded by four companions; a man and woman on board are waving to him, craning over the piled crates. The musician is strumming one of the songs of the island, a song of farewell.

So, with the sad, slow melodies of the island music haunting our minds, let us leave the Isle of Tranquillity. We are going, not with too great an eagerness for re-union with the familiar things of home, but with too strong a regret for the loss of that simplicity and harmony of life that we are forsaking.

We are taking with us the memory of many smiles, many kindnesses, many rich personalities, many acquaintances, and a few friends ; in exchange we shall have the old familiar things of normal life that now seem so remote.

The home-bound wanderer who has travelled with an unprejudiced mind and an open heart must inevitably discover that the pleasure of the return is tempered by some degree of regret for the loss of new-found beauties. In moments of retrospect the memory of a smile, or of a kindness, or of some tranquil hour of perfect sunlit harmony will engender a vague sadness that one is loath to dispel. Only the dyspeptic, the misanthrope, and the superior person can return to the normal with unalloyed satisfaction. We are neither dyspeptic nor misanthropic nor superior, so that our journey back to the north is tinged with vague regret and a sense of loss.

Back to the mirk and clatter of London we come, to the old familiar things that somehow seem to have faded during our absence. Even one's favourite Kelim seems to have lost its colour ; yet we know that the fault lies in ourselves rather than in any omission by a faithful retainer ! There is a sense of desolation in London this rainy summer day, almost an unfriendliness ; or at the very least a lack of enthusiasm for our return !

Until the dog reappears.

If you have ever been greeted by a dog who has been pining for your presence during months of absence ; a dog who on sight of you so completely loses control of his tail that his whole tempestuous body vibrates and dithers with the violence of the emotion expressed by that appendage ; whose more-than-human soul glows in his eyes with an intensity that puts your own vapid enthusiasms to shame—then surely will your sense of loss and desolation be dispelled, and the colour of your old life be revived.

It is reviving for us now, in spite of the one small tragedy that mars our return. We search for our other and smaller friend, the fly, and at last we find him, stiff and lifeless, dried up, crouching in a corner of a window ledge, where he had crawled in hopeless quest of sunshine and warmth : a victim of an English summer !

We shall give him a fitting burial in the window box ; and his requiem shall be one of the saddest of the dirges of Majorca !

THE END.

AFTERWORD

IN the hope that you did enjoy this book as much as I did, what if you wanted to retrace their journey today ? I have done, and the same thrill of discovery is there. It would, of course, be foolish to expect no change in an island that can now be reached from London in a two-hour flight ; but there are still so many opportunities to discover what Gordon West called " the exquisite peace of Mallorca ". In fact he would applaud the measures being taken to restrict development, to protect the island and its natural beauty : in the mountains, for example, the pilgrim ways and the walls and terraces are being lovingly restored and spectacular walks abound.

The special rhythm of the wheels of the Mallorcan train no longer takes you as far as Arta, but the old part of Palma has kept its charm and the Caves retain the pillared pattering of their deep mysteries, though the lighting is electric now, not torch. Gordon West and the Spirit would not be disappointed if they returned, and even now they'd find some of the *fondas* they visited. The secret of it all is to explore, as they did, at a leisurely pace.

But what else do we know about them ? Of Gordon West, only, from his conversation with the reluctant little passport official, that he was born in Guildford : but after a great deal of dogged detective work I discovered Book Trust who gave the information summarized on page 3 of this book. The Spirit's name turned out to be Mary ; and as for Don Juan, well, at least I had the address which he asked Gordon West to print in order to bring him more work. Towns and villages on the island tend to change street names and house numbers, and his was no exception. But a lot of footwork and a little guesswork led me to the door. From a local estate agent who'd known him, I discovered he was also a well-respected *amo*, someone who looked after various *fincas* in the area. And I saw the handwritten certificate of his birth on 6th June, 1882, and the filled-in certificate of his death on 14th October, seventy years later.

And I promise you I did see a beige mule just outside Deia the other day, and when I stroked her and whispered " Roja " in her ear, she gazed at me with big gold-brown eyes and most definitely smiled.

LEONARD PEARCEY

Perfume From Provence

Lady Fortescue

In the early 1930s, Winifred Fortescue and her husband, Sir John Fortescue, left England and settled in Provence, in a small stone house amid olive groves, on the border of Grasse. Their exodus had been caused partly by ill health, but mostly for financial reasons, for it was in the period between the wars when it was cheaper to live in France than in England.

Almost at once they were bewitched, by the scenery, by their garden – an incredible terraced landscape of vines, wild flowers, roses and lavender – and above all by the charming, infuriating, warm-hearted and wily Provençals. The house – called the Domaine – was delightful but tiny, and at once plans were put in hand to extend it over the mountain terraces. Winifred Fortescue's witty and warm account of life with stone masons, builders, craftsmen, gardeners, and above all her total involvement with the everyday events of a Provençal village, made *Perfume From Provence* an instant bestseller that went into several editions and became a famous and compulsive book for everyone who has ever loved France, most especially Provence.

0 552 99479 0

BLACK SWAN

Sunset House

Lady Fortescue

The sequel to the bestselling *Perfume From Provence*.

Winifred Fortescue and her husband, Sir John Fortescue, moved to Provence in the early 1930s. There they converted an old stone farmhouse into a graceful and idyllic home – the Domaine.

For two years after his death, Lady Fortescue, still a comparatively young woman, continued to live in the Domaine, years that were not altogether happy. Then, visiting a friend, she came across a small, near-derelict house set amidst thickets of wild lavender, magenta gladioli, and trailing sweet peas. She fell instantly in love with it, and thus began a new and happy chapter of her life.

With the help of her dear friend and neighbour, 'Mademoiselle', she set about trying to purchase the property from a complicated and cunning 'Mafia' of local Provençals – and then, once more, she began the heartwarming, frustrating, funny, and altogether delightful process of transforming a small Provençal cottage into a home and creating a breathtaking garden down the side of the mountain.

She called it SUNSET HOUSE.

0 552 99557 6

BLACK SWAN

There's Rosemary, There's Rue

Lady Fortescue

In 1935 a book called *Perfume From Provence* was published which instantly became a bestseller, rocketing its gentle, charming author almost overnight to fame and success. The book, telling of Sir John and Lady Fortescue's life in Provence, also gave tantalising glimpses of what had gone before and, finally, after Sir John's death, Lady Fortescue wrote the full story of her life, and most particularly of her meeting and marriage with John Fortescue.

Here is the fascinating, nostalgic recreation of another era, of her excitement as an actress before the First World War, of her meeting with the man she was to marry, and of their first home together in Windsor Castle during the reign of King George V and Queen Mary. Many famous names of the times drift across her pages which are warm, witty, and altogether delightful.

This is the story of the woman behind *Perfume From Provence*.

0 552 99558 4

BLACK SWAN

A SELECTION OF FINE WRITING
AVAILABLE FROM BLACK SWAN

THE PRICES SHOWN BELOW WERE CORRECT AT THE TIME OF GOING TO PRESS. HOWEVER TRANSWORLD PUBLISHERS RESERVE THE RIGHT TO SHOW NEW RETAIL PRICES ON COVERS WHICH MAY DIFFER FROM THOSE PREVIOUSLY ADVERTISED IN THE TEXT OR ELSEWHERE.

☐ 99493 6	COAST TO COAST	*Andy Bull*	£5.99
☐ 99537 1	GUPPIES FOR TEA	*Marika Cobbold*	£5.99
☐ 99587 8	LIKE WATER FOR CHOCOLATE	*Laura Esquivel*	£5.99
☐ 99563 0	THE SUNDAY TIMES BLACK SWAN LITERARY QUIZ BOOK	*ed. Philip Evans*	£3.99
☐ 99508 8	FIREDRAKE'S EYE	*Patricia Finney*	£5.99
☐ 99479 0	PERFUME FROM PROVENCE	*Lady Fortescue*	£5.99
☐ 99557 6	SUNSET HOUSE	*Lady Fortescue*	£5.99
☐ 99558 4	THERE'S ROSEMARY, THERE'S RUE	*Lady Fortescue*	£6.99
☐ 99438 3	A PLACE FOR US	*Nicholas Gage*	£5.99
☐ 99467 7	MONSIEUR DE BRILLANCOURT	*Clare Harkness*	£4.99
☐ 99369 7	A PRAYER FOR OWEN MEANY	*John Irving*	£6.99
☐ 99364 6	VIDEO NIGHT IN KATHMANDU	*Pico Iyer*	£5.99
☐ 99507 X	THE LADY AND THE MONK	*Pico Iyer*	£5.99
☐ 99585 1	FALLING OFF THE MAP	*Pico Iyer*	£5.99
☐ 99505 3	TRUTH TO TELL	*Ludovic Kennedy*	£7.99
☐ 99542 8	SWEET THAMES	*Matthew Kneale*	£5.99
☐ 99569 X	MAYBE THE MOON	*Armistead Maupin*	£5.99
☐ 99501 0	ROTTEN TIMES	*Paul Micou*	£5.99
☐ 99481 2	SIDE BY SIDE	*Isabel Miller*	£4.99
☐ 99504 5	LILA	*Robert Pirsig*	£5.99
☐ 99506 1	BETWEEN FRIENDS	*Kathleen Rowntree*	£5.99
☐ 99529 0	OUT OF THE SHADOWS	*Titia Sutherland*	£5.99
☐ 99470 7	THE RECTOR'S WIFE	*Joanna Trollope*	£5.99
☐ 99495 2	A DUBIOUS LEGACY	*Mary Wesley*	£5.99
☐ 99591 6	A MISLAID MAGIC	*Joyce Windsor*	£4.99

All Black Swan Books are available at your bookshop or newsagent, or can be ordered from the following address:

Black Swan Books,
Cash Sales Department
P.O. Box 11, Falmouth, Cornwall TR10 9EN

UK and B.F.P.O. customers please send a cheque or postal order (no currency) and allow £1.00 for postage and packing for the first book plus 50p for the second book and 30p for each additional book to a maximum charge of £3.00 (7 books plus).

Overseas customers, including Eire, please allow £2.00 for postage and packing for the first book plus £1.00 for the second book and 50p for each subsequent title ordered.

NAME (Block Letters) ....

ADDRESS ....

....